A COUNTRY DO

My 72nd birthday, Sunday lunch – 2001.
Mari, Elin, Richard (Kellett), Rhys,
Sam, Josh, Nathalie, Gwyn and Owen.

A Country Doctor's Diary

by

J. GWYN THOMAS

GWASG GEE
DENBIGH

ISBN 0 7074 0351 0

PRINTED AND BOUND BY
GWASG GEE, DENBIGH, N. WALES
PUBLISHERS, PRINTERS AND BOOKBINDERS

Contents

Many thanks to the following for reading the script, correcting and bowderizing much of it:–

Mrs. Haf Williams, B.A.
Mr. Gwyn Dodd, B.A.
Mr. Paddy Bennatt, B.A.
Mr. Edward Lloyd, B.A.(Law)
Mr Rhys Thomas, B.Sc.
Mrs. Gwyneth Stringfellow
(ex Medical Postgraduate Secretary for typing the original)

There is only one untrue tale included.
You may guess – no prize is offered!

Preface

It is a singular privilege to be invited to preface and introduce this autobiography. The title in some aspects is misleading in that unlike Samuel Pepys'' famous diary of daily experiences and comments this relates in a most engaging fashion episodes in his life, often outlandish, but reflecting the realities of a busy family doctor's work.

The narrative and style of writing is engaging and eminently readable even compulsive; festooned with much humour. It depicts an autobiographical tale of the relative innocence of childhood to the mischievous adventures and often reckless – even irresponsible forays of adolescence – and young manhood; but later nurturing into a deeply caring physician showing tolerance and empathy with his medical flock and the human race in general. This is usually camouflaged by light-hearted banter and a bluff Falstaffian presence – in short an accomplished raconteur.

Medical practice has changed immensely during recent decades in Britain: – from the days when the family doctor was wise adviser, trusted confidant and friend commanding respect and loyalty, to the present where the general practitioner sadly has to be content with high technology and political bureaucracy; with a tendency for the patient to become a number rather than a person and where mutual trust is being eroded. In this volume it is manifest that the author during his career has managed to embrace both ends of the spectrum without losing that intimate doctor-patient relationship. Despite a busy schedule he has also found time to engage in medical education and politics which he relishes.

On a more personal note it is clear in the text that he is immensely proud of his heritage. Quite rightly he pays tribute to his rich family medical tradition – three generations of family doctors and eminent persons in the extended family. He holds his father, the late Doctor John in high regard and regrets he has failed to emulate his father's poetical talent – although he has tried the odd 'englyn' with no success. Most of all he is enormously proud of his close family and admits that he is blessed with a lovely wife and colleague Doctor Mari who quietly controls his exuberance.

Finally, he records his good fortune of having practiced his art within his own 'milltir sgwâr' and now in his retirement he can expend much energy gardening, fishing and minding other people's business; also that he is now free to do so, kiss his ex-patients on Denbigh High Street.

This is a fascinating and entertaining book highly recommended for bedtime reading and as an antidote to boredom.

Robert Owen

CHAPTER 1

Childhood

It must have been an unusual Georgian home where I was brought up, in comparison with others. On the cellar floor was the kitchen where the maid and washer-woman worked - the latter on Mondays, at her tub and boiler. The maids were, in the latter years, ex-North Wales Asylum patients who would live in, in the attic, and earn ten shillings a week. The last one, Jane, had cooked for Royalty before becoming ill. At one time there were two maids and, after one of them was sacked, the remaining one told my mother that the other used to spit into my mother's tea as she carried the tray upstairs to the bedroom! Before the last war, there were also two successive nursemaids, both Danish - to care for the three children.

The ground floor was behind the front door which led into the hallway where, in those days, one of the two telephones were positioned, the other in my parents' bedroom. Each member of the family was expected to answer the phone and make notes in the 'Call Book' for my father to read. Often we would have to call him, to the phone, from his surgery at the back of the house. The waiting room led to his consulting room which was heated by a gas fire it had gaslight at first, as did the consulting room - cum-dispensary, though there the heating was by a smelly, round, portable paraffin stove. He had a low leather couch for the patients to lie on, a nice leather-top desk and a small stool. The patients' records were held on pink or blue simple cards called 'Lloyd Georges'. The colour was determined by your sex. On a shelf above the records were specimens of various sorts. I recall a flat worm, a round worm and a foetus, all in glass bottles and methylated spirits. Big drawers held cotton wool, bandages and splints. Rows of ointments, concentrated medicines to be diluted before dispensing with water carried from the kitchen periodically and ten different coloured aspirins (for fail-safe reasons) sat in their jars or Winchester bottles. There was no legally-required 'Poisons Cupboard' but he kept a Dangerous Drugs Register.

As a small boy, I can recall finding Professor T. Glyn Davies, a close friend of my father lying in the dark, on the couch, asleep. My father had passed a catheter to bypass his probably enlarged prostate gland and he had gone to sleep with relief. Professor T Gwynn Jones of Aberystwyth, the Welsh Literary giant, used to call for a chat with him at times. He had married a Denbigh girl. Other Welsh national figures, Dr Kate Roberts, Mr Gwilym R. Jones and Mr Mathonwy Hughes were later to become his patients. In the Llanrwst National Eisteddfod of 1951 he was to win the first prize for an epitaph to T. Rowland Hughes. A collection of his poems *Y Doctor Tomos* was published a year after his death.

We spoke only Welsh to him but English to my Holywell-born mother. She was a dental surgeon, with a surgery on the first floor between the bedrooms. She was the third of five children of a wealthy, in both terms of cash and literary skills, general practitioner, while my father was one of eleven children of the village postmaster in Cyffylliog - a JP, Deacon, quack-chemist and dentist. Both of my Grandfathers had died fairly young, my paternal one with a stroke. I have a fairly large collection of my father's letters, from the trenches in the First World War, as a Second Lieutenant in the Machine Gun Corps.While convalescing from shrapnel wounds the King awarded him the Military Cross. Later my father went for a course in Medicine at Liverpool University, where my mother was studying Dentistry. They married and came to Denbigh in 1925. For the first twenty years they remained very close, often giving concerts when he would sing and she play the harp. But things - for some reason unknown to we children - changed. They slept in different rooms. He was always having his breakfast just before we had lunch and was known as 'Deryn y Nos' (bird of the night), as he never went to bed before 2 a.m. If he saw a bedroom light on in a patient's home, as he drove past, he would call to see if all was well!

My brother Deri was born in 1927, my sister Gwenllian in 1931 and I was the middle one, born in Denbigh Infirmary where I was to deliver 1,500 babies with the help of the midwives, during my medical career. The Maternity Department was closed in the 1970s as the numbers, and thus our skills, fell.

As a boy I shall later describe my employment in two shops nearby to make some cash for cigarettes and the cinema but I also had to go through the trauma of asking my father for pocket money. I would stand by his side as he ate a meal and read the 'Faner' or 'Cymro'. I would draw his attention to my presence by a small cough and then utter my request - not demand! He would make me stand there for a few minutes then go into his waistcoat pocket or to a tin in his roll-top desk and give me the sixpence. You'd have thought I was going to buy condoms not Woodbines!

I can recall being in bed with some infection when I fancied a small bottle of dandelion and burdock pop. I had asked the maid to call next door to get a bottle from the shop and to book it down to my father, a domestic habit in those days, but I had never tried it before - or since! My father came to see how I was, saw the bottle, asked its origin, then called me, "You thief!" in Welsh. I still cringe at the episode.

One autumn evening, my father was driving alone over the Denbigh moors and felt unwell. He stopped at the Sportsman's Arms and was given a whiskey by the landlady, a patient of his. As he drove on he took his hands off the steering wheel to light a Woodbine and must have swerved a little. A policeman following in a car, stopped him and made him walk on the straight line in the middle of the road. He fortunately passed all right. It quite upset him. The police in those days knew and would recognise all the local doctor's cars and he was almost a tea-totaller.

He was so dedicated to his work and local friends that he never returned to his Alma Mater in Liverpool. I did take him to see my mother there following an operation - he drank his warmed up tea in a flask at the bedside and had traversed the Mersey Tunnel for the first time. While in a Chinese Restaurant in Hereford, when we were returning from a visit to his old friend, Rev. Emrys Cleaver in Cardiff, he handed the waiter a sixpence from his waistcoat and asked for a *Denbigh Free Press*! He was well retired at that time.

He used to write his best Welsh short poems on the frosted glass door while sitting on the toilet. The stale smell of his cigarettes and his dogs in the car was heaven to me. He kept the two white terriers in the car to keep it warm when he returned from a house call. The car was warm but steamed up. He taught me Welsh folk songs as I travelled with him as a young man. Any rabbit he shot or hit with the car he would skin and in the middle of the night arrive home to cook it for the dogs - with a stink throughout the house. One morning my mother came down to the cellar kitchen and found that he had painted the walls in the night.

Sometimes he would be found tidying the front garden by torchlight, wearing his spats and trilby.Our seat in chapel was near the door so I could get him out quietly if he was needed in an emergency. I recall one occasion when a leading local man had died suddenly in the Deacon's seat in another chapel, and I had run there to call him out, and on another occasion when a distinguished local lady had telephoned to say her husband was shaking all over. She did not recognise the 'delirium tremens' of an alcoholic.

I was frightened of our Chapel Minister as a child - a big man in black in the pulpit high above me. However, many years later we became friends, especially when I had to do a rectal examination on him. The tables had turned.

Rightly or wrongly, I was my parents' doctor. My father was an in-patient with a bad chest and confusion at the Infirmary for 2 years (unheard of these days), and I saw his chest infection was pretty serious so called a Consultant Geriatrician to see him to avoid any family squabbles. She advised me to let him die! I fought hard and kept him alive but completely disorientated for a further six months. I often wonder, "for whose sake?" My relationship with him - like that of my brother - was that we adored him and were frightened of him. He showed very little affection for us. He did buy me a scooter as a ten year old and a car a year after qualifying. That was it! He, as one of eleven children, only had an orange for Christmas.

I remember very little of my very early childhood except being attacked by a cockerel in the back yard, which was to give me a phobia of feathers for 50 years. I fancied myself as a tight- rope walker after being to a local circus and tried it on the taut clothes line, using the pole as a balance. I fell of course, half way across, on to the sandpit. I still have some sand and grit in the scar on my left knee.

We cooked chips in the garden on a bonfire - in a frying pan with stale fat and sold them wrapped in Bronco toilet paper at a half a penny a pack. We kept the fire going with paraffin, which got into the chips. Our friends still remind us of those chips.

When I was about 8 years old, Deri and I made some pocket money (which was very scarce) brushing snow off the pavement of houses in Chapel Street. One person recently recalled how one lady refused to pay and so we put the snow back! The same happened to our Chapel front - Capel Mawr.

I can recall Miss Annie Jones, Miss Nellie and Miss Josephine Jones - teachers in the Primary Frongoch School. I was sent there when 3 years old with my brother Deri. Miss Annie was later a patient of mine.

It must have been most embarrassing for me - though I don't recall the emotion - when my mother brought my unfolded pyjamas to the school and I was made to fold them before the class. It probably taught me a lesson; I don't think she had to tell me again. Looking back, it was a rather cruel thing to do to a child of any age. It was she who had to discipline us over the years as my father was too occupied by his work - or couldn't be bothered. I can remember being one of a team of bullies there and swapping safety pins for girls' knicker elastic to make catapults. (Maybe that was the reason we were sent to a private school when seven years old, which had 6 boys and 30 sources of knicker elastic!)

I cannot understand my father sending us to a private school in Denbigh - Fairholme - from the age of 7 to 10 years. He had been a teacher in a village school before going to the trenches in the 1914-1918 War. However, I had extra Arithmetic at the Headmistress's home on Saturday mornings, which paid off as I passed the Scholarship to the County School of 360 pupils, when 10 years old. I had also learnt the Lord's Prayer in English, to play hockey, and knit! All very useful! For some reason my sister was not given the opportunity of private education until later.

It was about this time that I began to spend most of my spare time working in a greengrocer's - Eirwen's - close to my home. All the school holidays and Saturdays I would spend time serving fruit and vegetables and I learnt how to make wreaths. I was paid one shilling or a bag of damaged fruit, which I dutifully handed to my mother. I learnt much about people and got to know a lot of them. I would go to her home after Sunday School and sing as she played the piano. We had a good, healthy friendship over many years, until she finally died as a patient of mine.

We used to prepare orange boxes of greengroceries for Scout Troops from all over Britain - there would be 20,000 Scouts at Bryn

Bach camp - a lovely valley five miles away. Robert Owen's grocers nearby used to deliver groceries, by van, there and the greengroceries and I travelled with it, to leave in the shop in the camp and to be picked up by the Scouts.

Sometimes I would travel with a grocery delivery to the surrounding farms. We would stop at the mill in Llanrhaeadr. Hywel Owen, (the driver and owner) would collect four eggs and bacon from the van and the miller's wife would produce a most excellent fry up over an old cast iron fire place. Maybe, as it was war time, I enjoyed it all the more.

One Sunday morning a patient of my fathers was aggressively knocking on the front door as my father slept. I answered it. It was a man who was always drunk - so much so that when I was in practice I told him not to come to the surgery except in the afternoons as he was less drunk then. He used to sing in the pubs and be encouraged by free tankards of beer. He told me that dislocated his shoulder. I was about 16 years old. I refused to disturb my father; so he demanded that I restore the shoulder. After much persuasion, I grabbed it, twisted it and 'clunk' it went back. We were close friends ever after. I went to his funeral, from the surgery on a Saturday lunch time, to find the church pervaded, not by the smell of incense but of stale beer from his pals.

As I got older and needed more cash for fags or cinema, I went to work nearby in the Radio Shop - again serving at the counter, charging batteries and doing simple repairs, until called up for National Service. My employment for 2/6d a day in Llew Williams' radio shop was really to keep it open during the day in school holidays and on Saturdays while Llew Williams himself worked in a munitions' factory and the Auxillary Fire Service, while his father, a local miller, took charge in the evenings and repaired radios upstairs. The shop, on the corner, has now gone. Friends of Mr Robert H Williams would call in to chat around the open coal fire upstairs. I would enjoy listening to tales of farming and game-keeping. One day a Mrs Annie Ellis called in with a 6 valve radio set to dump. I checked it out, got it going and she told me to keep it. I took it to a car sales'auction in the Smithfield, sold it for £9 on condition I set it up with an aerial, on a farm. This money was the beginning of a bank account which has never been in the red since, by good fortune and care. I have a nice plaque on our bedroom wall, from her family, received on my retirement. She herself, poor woman, had Alzheimer's at the time and was in a home.

This is the period, too, when I would join my cousin Medwyn at Cyffylliog for the occasional week, staying in my grandmother's shop with her spinster daughter Ceri. It was always great fun. We would go poaching rabbits with snares, or fish by hand under the stones in the River Clywedog. I knew every stone in the river near the village - as my father must have done before me. A Liverpool doctor had a house, Merllyn, just outside the village and we would tease their English daughters. Nearby lived 'Elis y Go' in his corrugated iron hut in the woods. It was said he suffered from shell shock. We would throw stones at his hut to create a noise and he would swear at us - the same idiom each time. Part of it would be, "Rho dy drwyn yn dy din a chwistlo!"

The shop sold everything - groceries, boots, cartridges and suits. They made their own bread. Medwyn's father would heat a bakehouse oven with burning sticks, while kneading the dough nearby, before putting the product in tins and sliding them into the heated and cleaned oven. Corn seeds were sold from the cellar, in competition with one of the sons who lived in Bryn Saith Marchog. Medwyn's father, who ran the shop, would catch a mouse in the sacks and present it to me from his closed hand. He was a very kindly man, a Deacon and Justice of the Peace, just like his father before him. He had a long-drawn-out illness, a gradual creeping paralysis. While a medical student I arranged for him to see a Neurologist in Cardiff of no avail. My father attended his post mortem at Llangwyfan Hospital, to see the unusual diagnosis of Platybasia.

Going to Chapel and Sunday School were a must in Cyffylliog. I believe we upset the place by our behaviour. Aunty Ceri used to play the Chapel organ. We cousins were invited to the Vicarage for tea on one occasion. I can't understand why. We all started to giggle at the table and had to leave the unfinished tea - and the house! I recall a Mr John Bumby holding Medwyn's brother Huw by an ear and telling him off for, "laughing like a squirrel in chapel, and his father a deacon!"

We learned the hard way of Nature there. I remember Medwyn tying a sheepdog to a tree and shooting it, at the request of a farmer. He also robbed a thrush's nest and squashed the eggs on my head.

Everyone assembled on the village square after chapel to talk. One of the local girls recalled recently that I had offered her a Kit-Kat if I could see her 'private parts'.

It was during these wonderful holidays in Cyffylliog that we used to sing at the old harmonium in my Aunty Kit's and Uncle Hugh's house. My local cousins had good voices, especially Beryl and Medwyn. Their mother taught the daughters of the Lloyd family - who were neighbours at Maes Aleg - to sing and later to become well known Welsh singers and harpists, Meinir, Morfydd and Bronwen Lloyd.

Sometimes another cousin from Denbigh, whose father was a local Cyffylliog man and bank cashier, would join us on the holiday - his name is Gwyn Lloyd. He was later to obtain a science degree in Bangor, worked for the Ministry of Agriculture at the Pest Control Department and wrote a standard text book on 'The Red Fox'. With similar interests - fishing and rabbiting - we enjoyed his company. His brother, Emyr, was in charge of the fishing on the Brenig Reservoir and again was a knowledgeable nature-lover. We saw little of the other Cyffylliog cousins, at this time, as they were younger.

My academic career was poor in the County School. I was kept in detention by Mr Stanley Jones until 5 p.m. daily for about two years - to write lines and poetry, mainly to try to improve my writing. Little did he think that my future was in medicine! Often we would tie three pencils together and write three times "I must remember to remember and remember not to forget!" or something equally as daft, during lunch time, and handing it in after sitting for 10 minutes in the classroom. On one occasion I told Stan that I had to go to see the Headmaster - "Boss" as we called him. He advised me to go to gargle first as I stank of Woodbines.

We gave the French teacher, who was the Deputy Head and stepmother to the late High Court Judge William Mars Jones, a tough time in French each day! She had recently arrived, from an English Girls' Private School. At one internal exam period a boy had stolen a copy of the following day's French exam question paper. I bought a copy for a shilling, did the paper on stolen writing paper in Eirwen's home and handed it in at the end of the exam the following day. Normally expecting a mark such as 10 to 20 per cent, I got 90 per cent. What little sense one had! I was told to resit the paper in the Head's room - and qualified for 10 per cent.

The Gravestone of Hugh Davies and his sister at Cynwyd.
(Bone Setters) Distant relation.

Author's father, Dr. J. G. Thomas with Sister Lee and Sister Haf.

My father never saw that term's report! For some reason I was not punished as far as I can recall. The cat was never out of the bag (nor the cane, for some reason)!

In the earliest days at school we were beginning to learn about sex. A Miss Stocken used to wear a low-cut blouse and we would encourage her to lean over our arithmetic work so we could have a peep. Then another would sit cross-legged at the front. I can recall one girl making a drawing of a sanitary towel so I could understand how some girls became 'unwell'. We came across used condoms in Bryn Park on Mondays, left by the American soldiers over the weekend. Unaware of any danger we would carry some and pull them over the door knobs in Post Office Lane, near school.

Our Headquarters of the St John Ambulance Cadets was above the showers of the USA Officers' Mess and the shower equipment was supervised by a Corporal Shinsook. Through knot-holes in the floor we would watch him canoodling with women - including one of our fellow pupils. He smoked a big fat cigar between whiles! I don't believe any of we boys went that far.

Potato picking, during term time, was a good dodge during the war at Mr Foulkes Jones' farm in Llandyrnog. For 6d an hour we picked them - throwing most of them at each other and at cyclists on the road nearby. My brother and I also had to pick some at home on Saturdays, from seeds that my father had planted in a plot behind St Mary's Church. We hated doing it - and for free! He had obtained a large number of packets of tea from his mother's village shop and also salted butter during the rationing, storing them in a large Chinese cedar chest. The food stank and tasted of the scent.

Petrol rationing was very little problem for my father but my mother's allowance, as a dentist, was very small. As she garaged her car in the Foundry Garage Yard, the proprietor allowed her some extra to visit one sister in Holywell and the other in the burning city of Liverpool.

Having a maid gave my mother the opportunity to practice her dentistry in a room on the first floor. She would be quite busy. Any difficult extraction and she would call my father to give a pull! We were quite used to hearing people yell from her surgery in a room between the bedrooms.

At break times in school we boys met at a hollow in the school field to smoke and drink Bovril or Vimto. The caretaker - Peter

Williams - was a very co-operative friend to me and I would go for a smoke in the boiler house - as he puffed on his pipe. In later years he became a patient of mine. At other times, we would hurry to the school football fields at three o'clock on Fridays and have a smoke in the changing hut before the teacher arrived.

Mr Harding, or Jack Tar as he was called, was supervising the soccer when a boy fractured his leg. A few weeks earlier I had captained the Denbigh St. John Cadets, who had won the Twiston Davies Cup for First Aid in Cardiff, so took charge and organised things. I told others to bring the gate to the boy as a stretcher and carried him to the roadway to wait for the ambulance. I well recall Jack Tar saying, "A little knowledge is a dangerous thing, boy." About ten years later he apologised for this and asked to come on my list of patients. He died a few years later while playing golf.

It was about this time that someone had stolen the scissors from the school first aid box on one of the corridors. The Head, Mr W A Evans, announced this to the school assembly and pronounced that Mr Stanley Jones, a stretcher bearer from the First World War and I were to be the only two to go into the box infuture - a big ego trip!

On another occasion the music teacher, a dear Miss Morris, asked me to organise a musical concert. This I did, but during an interval I had arranged for two pals to gallop into the school assembly hall dressed as a comic cow. She told me off and said she would never ask me to arrange such a thing again.

The County School Eisteddfod was fun. I was elected, by my peers in Myddleton House, to train and conduct its choir to sing 'O Lovely Peace'. Fortunately Dorothy Kirk, later to become Head of Music in a girls' private school in Liverpool, now a local talented organist, was the pianist. I was delighted to hear the adjudicator, Rev Emrys Cleaver, declare the Myddleton Choir had won, "although the choir was singing in 3:4 time but the conductor conducting in 2:6 time!"

I would have a go at anything in school in the sporting line, though was not much good at it. I recall being in goal in a house match when the ball rolled into the net between my legs; I was afraid of the cricket ball and so stood at long-stop. I ran cross-country quite well but excelled at the sack race, egg and spoon race and putting the weight. I 'put on weight' 50 years later! At break time, I would join others at a sweet shop - Mrs Addies - for milk and doughnuts and chat to her invalid husband through the small window to his bedroom.

A Miss Jenkins, class Geography teacher, used to come to us for supper every Sunday night. Because of this, I was forced to do homework at a desk in my mother's dental surgery at least once a week. School Certificate exam results were poor - 4 credits and 2 passes. No foreign language, which was needed to get into Medical School, an ambition of mine from childhood. In spite of the fact that I had been kept down in Form IV and V for a second year, I was allowed to get into Form VI Science to do Physics, Chemistry and Biology. The teaching, in the two latter subjects, was poor. The teacher in Biology had come back from the Army Tank Corps in Africa and I realise, with hindsight, had pre-senile dementia, alcoholism, or post-traumatic stress syndrome. The Chemistry teacher had a very weak personality, certainly for teaching boys, and a few years later she sadly hanged herself.

One winter in snow, I recall pulling a dead sheep down from home to school on a sledge. It had been left by a thoughtful farmer - and we dissected it in Form VI for weeks. I was proud that my dissection of some of the spinal nerves of a rabbit was on display for years, pickled in formaldehyde. Two years later I was to get the prize - the Samuel Brother's Scholarship, in the Medical School - for those three subjects I had failed in the Higher School Certificate. The two years in the RAF as a Nursing Orderly - a Corporal for six months - did me good.

Never once did my father commend me. In fact, on one occasion he looked at a term's report and threw it on the floor in the dining room saying, "Comic Cuts!" - a children's comic at the time. I cannot understand this - he did comment to one of his peers once, I am told, that I was doing all right in the RAF and College.

Our mother had an Austin Seven - BCA 435 - a number known to everyone, as Deri and I would borrow it when 17 years old. I had been taught to drive by a postman in a Post Office van, driving on his delivery round on the Denbigh Moors and passed the Test, when six days past the 17 year old mark. We became reasonable mechanics, even changing the back axle half-shaft, which we broke quite often by driving through fields chasing rabbits, a habit taught to us by my father, who would open the front windscreen of his Morris with his shotgun at the ready and chase rabbits in the headlights of his car at night - food for his two white terriers. I used to enjoy going on the rounds with him in a car, which was stinking of the dogs and cigarettes, but he'd sit for hours in the patient's house talking while I sat in the car with the dogs and rugs to keep me warm. His was a tough life, up late at night, opening farm and mountain gates and often having to put on snow chains before starting off. Half his patients paid him in kind - bacon, eggs, buttermilk - until 1948 when the National Health Service started.

I would watch him suturing wounds or giving a general anaesthetic in the Denbighshire Infirmary while Mr Owen Jones, from Wrexham, would be doing a Caesarean operation, my father reciting poetry and Mr Owen Jones singing hymns. He attended every delivery and taught me to do the same. He lost one mother, with a ruptured womb, in a cottage in Panton Hall.

About a year after the end of the War an organisation was set up, the World Friendship Association, to encourage children of all nations to meet and understand each other. My school had five volunteers, all boys. The Headmaster called us to his room with instructions and said, "Gwyn, you are in charge." I was probably 17 years old, the others younger. We were to be detailed off to stay with families in Amsterdam. After a rough crossing, I remember being very sick, especially when Ronald advised me to tie a piece of bacon on a string and swallow it! We were met at the station and taken off by the families. My host was a furniture constructor with two daughters - not very beautiful. They were very kind and took me to see the bulb fields, Machen, Delft and Scheveningen Beach. Everyone was amazed that I could pronounce the latter. I still feel guilty that we did not have the girls back to stay. As far as I recall, it was an interesting holiday.

An occasional treat was to cycle to the Creamery in Llandyrnog to a free film show given by the Ministry of Information. I would sit with a local boy, Clwyd, a school pal of mine. The films were mainly educational. The River Clwyd, near the village, was also the local swimming pool where I was nearly drowned once while swimming across the pool. I remember being pulled out and vomiting on the river bank. It was about this time that I excelled as a potato peeler. This I did in a Denbigh circus kitchen to get in free and later at Colwyn Bay National Eisteddfod, for the caterers, to get into the field free.

I had had free access to the cinema on Thursday nights, in my St. John's Cadet uniform, and made the most of it. I saw every film in the Scala, changing two to three times a week, for a few years. The only patient I had there was the Senior St. John's man, Mr Jack Humphreys, who had an epileptic fit in the toilet. Friday nights saw us in the St John's Ambulance Headquarters, practising.

In 1939 the National Eisteddfod came to Denbigh. A great deal of preparation had taken place. My father was elected, aged 48 years, as the Chairman of the Gorsedd Committee. It must have been a great delight to him, as it is to me to have the same post for the 2001 Eisteddfod being held here again. I recall selling plums, from a truck on my own at the Gorsedd and the main pavilion fields, for Eirwen. As I was trained to make wreaths, my father asked me to make an archway over the entrance to the Gorsedd Field in wreaths of poppies, saying 'Croeso ir orsedd'. It was a success.

A spin off from my father's Chairmanship was that I was able to sit with him in the front row of the pavilion on the Thursday, of August 1939, when Lloyd George played his usual role of President. The Second World War was coming, so he was very emotional and was spitting on to me as he became excited. One night the famous tenor David Lloyd, and others, came to my home after a concert. I sat on the stairs and could hear him and others singing in the sitting room, while my mother played the harp. He came out and caught me listening and encouraged me to sing a duet with him there and then. I had won a rosette for singing in Chapel, presented to me by the late Mrs Dryhurst Dodd when I was 8 years old. Sixty five years later she was conductor of the Denbigh Male Voice Choir.

Neither the Chair, which is now the Town Mayor's Seat, nor the Crown was won. The latter was used in the Colwyn Bay Eisteddfod in 1947, with the name Denbigh replaced by Colwyn Bay. It is now in the home of the winner's daughter, in Bangor.

A few days after the Eisteddfod we three children were taken, by our mother to a rented house in Llanfair Road in Abergele, for a week's holiday. My father had only taken one day off in 38 years of practice. One morning my mother spotted Lord Clwyd walking hurriedly to the station and she asked him how things were in Parliament. He replied that war was inevitable. I can recall the shock. I can also recall the shock the family suffered on hearing that the Thetis submarine had been sunk off Llandudno. I was standing in the back garden at home at the time.

We dug a trench in our sandpit and covered it with corrugated iron, concrete and soil, as a shelter from bombs. Only one fell, a mile outside the town, dropped by a German plane as it was making full speed for home, having dropped the others onto Liverpool. A number of our local Auxiliary Fire Service went with our fire tenders to help in Liverpool - Dei Wheway Davies, John Hywel Williams, 'Corporal' and Llewellyn Williams. It was great fun for we boys at this time, with Nissen huts on Rhyl Road and Llanerch Park, an anti-aircraft gun surrounded by sandbags in front of the high ground of the Castle and the Home Guard busy on Saturdays.

Most able-bodied men in the area not called up, for instance if in food production or farming, were in the Home Guard or served as an Air Raid Wardens. The Denbigh area was divided into two sections, the Town and the Country. Dr Duff was the Medical Officer for the town and my father promoted, from being a Second Lieutenant in the Machine Gun Corps in the 1914/18 War, to now being a Major - and Medical Officer for the farms and villages around. He sported a khaki uniform and flat cap and the Military Cross ribbon.

Mock fights took place between them on Saturdays and on one occasion he was captured and locked in a school nearby. He was, of course, being single-handed, on call at all times for his practice. An urgent call came for him while in the 'prison' and I can remember taking a message up to him at the school, where he was drinking tea and chatting to his captors!

As a 15 year old, on Saturdays I would be on call for the ambulance with Mr Len Pierce (Len Skell as he was known). It was a voluntary service and a cream ambulance would be used for live persons and a green one for corpses. These rules were important, mainly I suppose to prevent infection, just in the same way that District Nurses and Midwives were not allowed to lay out corpses, as was the convention, lest disease be carried. Ordinary District Nurses, or locally appointed ladies, were fit to do the ritualistic jobs of washing the corpse and stuffing cotton wool up every orifice, tying the jaw up and feet together.

The first corpse for me to see, when I was 14 years old, was an Italian Prisoner of War, who had been crushed by a tractor on the main road to the nearby village of Henllan. My father took me there. The next was a man who was lying on the hedge near a village, having shot the top of his head off after a domestic upheaval. The third was a dead tramp, found in a farmyard and put in a wheelbarrow. Len Skell and I transferred him to a stretcher, tied him to it, but omitted to tie the stretcher to the runners. As we pulled out of the farmyard slope the back door opened. Out ran the stretcher and body on to the farmyard.

CHAPTER 2

Early Years

My father would do a post mortem on those patients he chose, wearing his trilby, spats and rubber sheet. He had handled machine guns in the trenches in the 1914/18 War and seen enough corpses to harden him. Thoroughly. I watched him as I held the candle in the post mortem room, lay the body on a large, slate slab. He would cut open the chest, withdraw the heart, cut into it and declare, 'coronary thrombosis' with the aplomb of a football captain holding the winning cup at Wembley.

On one occasion I was called to 4 Rose Cottages in Henllan Street, in the green ambulance, where a dead middle-aged lady lay on two orange boxes, as a bed, and weighed 4 stone 4 lbs. We carried her to the hospital mortuary. An ensuing court case reprimanded the GP and the Poor Law Officer for neglecting her. The husband went to jail for neglecting her.

My father was the Father Christmas to the children of the staff of the Infirmary. After a pantomime he would distribute gifts, collected by Sister Emily Williams. I recall feeling so proud at being given a shaving stick for the first time, a change from Maltesers or Mars Bars - a sign of adulthood! Most of the nurses, especially the Sisters, were single women, and lived on the premises. Sister Jones and Matron Bundred were also always available as midwives.

The District Nurses were a Godsend and my father depended a lot on them as they were his patients' first port of call in Rhewl, Trefnant, Nantglyn, Llansannan and town. They too were single, dedicated ladies. Quite often I would see the Nantglyn nurse having a cup of coffee with my father, while he was having his breakfast, discussing some mutual problems. Some were qualified midwives and were salaried by a voluntary organisation.

I would stuff my nose into whatever I could - slaughter houses in Charnel's Well or Brynffynnon Farm in the town and watch pigs having their throat cut; but a real favourite was standing either watching or pumping the bellows in the Smithy behind Foundry Garage. Mr Jones, the owner of the garage, would remove his glass eye as a party piece to the horror of my friends. Mr Jones, the smith, was a skilled craftsman. He would allow me to smoke there, as long as I pumped the bellows. During the war he welded together what became known as the 'Duff Stretcher', designed by Dr Gordon Duff. It had two runners running fore and aft to travel on ice or snow and a bicycle wheel could be clamped to the centre of the runners so two men could run with the laden stretcher. I was tied to it on one occasion and lowered 75 yards down the face of our limestone quarry by ropes - to test it! He should have used one of his own two sons!

One day while walking over High Street, on the way home from school, I was challenged by Mr Jack Griffith, the coal man, to carry a sack of coal to a house near the castle on my back. I did it with pride. He spoke of it for a long time afterwards.

About once a month on Sundays a Mr Sutcliffe Kerr would attend the North Wales Mental Hospital, on the outskirts of the town, and perform pre-frontal leucotomies on patients who were not responding to the current treatment of Insulin coma, Electroconvulsant therapy, malaria, or a week's sleep on Paraldehyde. Two bore holes were drilled in the front of the skull under local anaesthetic. Then he would use a special blade to cut off part of the front of the brain. It was a great thrill to watch at the ringside with male nurses Mr Goronwy Davies and Mr Harry Vaughan 'in attendance'. They were both patients of mine when I returned to the town to practice. Later, I did two months' neurosurgery as a House Surgeon in Cardiff assisting Mr Charles Langmaid, Professor Lambert Rogers and the Senior Registrar, Mr Bryan Jennett, who was to become Professor of Neurosurgery in Glasgow and Dean of the Medical School - a world authority on 'Brain Death'.

On the way home from school we would call in the local Liberal Club to play snooker and billiards. The caretaker was the benign and pleasant Mr Parr. Later, in the evenings, the more experienced men would be playing as we watched and admired. One of the best was Mr Dei Edward Roberts, father of one of my pals then, Ken

(Ginge). He was the local newspaper reporter and known as 'The man about town'; another was teacher Mr Elwy Owen.

The features in the local Scala Cinema changed perhaps three times a week - Mr Rees followed by Mr Oliver Jones were the managers. As I said, I saw probably every show for three years, standing in a long queue of 200 yards to get in to one of the two nightly shows - except when 'on duty'!

In spite of having failed in the three subjects at Higher School Certificate, I was interviewed for admission to Liverpool Medical School, having passed the external exam in School Certificate Welsh as a foreign language. I had been expelled from the Welsh and Latin classes by Rev Edward Jones, as being uneducable! At the interview, with about ten academics, I was asked what my hobbies were. I replied "fishing" to which one asked me how I fished and I replied "by hand". I was asked to describe this and did so. When asked what effect the tickling had on the fish, guffaws were the response to my explanation that "it paralysed them with ecstasy." I felt sure I was in, but it was not to be; so I was called up for National Service in September 1947. I chose the RAF and after an intelligence test was allowed to follow my first choice, nursing.

While in school, on Sundays I spent some time with Alderman Hywel Owen, digging at the prehistoric caves in Cefn Meiriadog. A distant relation, he was Chairman of the County Council who, when Mayor of Denbigh, had been prosecuted for poaching salmon. Lying on our fronts, we chipped away, at the limestone walls. We found prehistoric bones and some pottery. It was quite exciting and encouraged my particular interest in anatomy, in later years. Some bits found their way to the National Museum of Wales and Chester Museum.

We were lucky in our Welsh Sunday School teacher, Mr Bob Edwards, Enterprise. He had served in the first World War and we would spend ten minutes reading the Bible with him in the gallery of the chapel, then talk about all sorts of things, reverent and irrelevant! About three-quarters of the members pursued academic careers afterwards, a general surgeon, a psychiatrist, a general practitioner, a dental surgeon and two ministers, who were brothers. Those two were religious swots even then. My brother and I would recite "God is Love" in front of the chapel after the morning service, while they would have learned a whole chapter and ad lib it. We were only a little jealous!

Occasionally my mother would be accompanied by my brother, sister and myself, to morning chapel. We found it most boring. Our seats were in the front, near a door, so we could signal to my father in the event that he was needed. We hardly understood a word as our Welsh was very poor. We had very few Welsh - or any other - conversations with our father and it was always in English with my mother. She was herself happier in English though her father, as I pointed out, was a great literary Welsh man with an enormous Welsh library.

On reflection, any Welsh I knew when I left home was that which we learned in Sunday School, as we heard no Welsh in the County School except when the Head read out the names of the people killed in the two wars and ended saying, "Mewn Angof ni chant fod." ("They will not be forgotten.")

Television was considered a sin at first. The Minister's wife kept hers under a cloth sheet so it could not be seen. She would come to my mother's sitting room and join her in smoking Du Mauriers, near the fireplace so the smoke went up the chimney. There were quite a few organisations in the town: Scouts, Air Training Corps, Army Cadets, Sea Cadets and St John's Ambulance Cadets. The Air Training Corps would go to Hawarden to see the planes; the Army cadets trained in the Drill Hall. I joined them but only for one night. It demanded too much discipline for me! I was quite happy in the St John's Cadets. Occasionally the Scouts would ask me to join them in Brynbach Scout Camp in case someone was injured.

As well as spending some holiday time in my father's village of Cyffylliog, I would spend a different sort of holiday in Holywell, my mother's home town. Her GP father had died when I was about two years old, leaving me 100 War Loan Shares, which were valueless in time but the thought was there. His son took over the practice and I would stay there in a large house with a permanent gardener, chauffeur, two maids and a visiting seamstress. It was quite a different experience from the Village Post Office. I would sit in my uncle's car on his practice rounds and was most upset, once, that he did not stop to help at a car accident at a cross roads. I have since learned that many GPs are unhappy about dealing with accidents. I came to enjoy dealing with them, at the site, taking charge as I often did. Doctors are hardly called to these scenes nowadays with trained Paramedics on the spot.

My uncle died in his fifties and Dr Gwilym Hooson from Denbigh, partnered later by Dr David Williams, a thrice Liberal Candidate for Parliament, took over on my youthful recommendation while in the RAF. It was later at my initiative, David was accepted as a Candidate, by the local Liberal Executive.

During the early years of the war, the town and schools took in evacuees who arrived at the station by train from Liverpool and later from Surrey and Guernsey. They assembled in the Modern School to be distributed by a local committee. Our mother came home with two sisters, Margaret and Sue McDonald, who attended Howell's School. Their father was the captain of the trans-atlantic ship Samaria and brought back Mars bars and other goodies from the USA. We became friendly, Deri in particular, with a red-headed Liverpool evacuee boy named Stan Beck and we three took to boxing. We built a ring in our garden and had two sets of gloves and a punchball. He was quite a bright boy. However we lost contact with him after his return to Hardwick Street in Liverpool. This is where the Royal Liverpool Hospital now stands. It was suggested to me recently that I put a reference to him in the 'Old Pals' column in the Liverpool Echo. I had eight replies! The first, a pal apologising to tell me that Stan was killed in the 1970s by a stolen car being chased by the Police in Liverpool. This was confirmed by others, including his widow, who sounded very nice - now a Mrs Brown. Another very Liverpool pal of his told me that he had gained a scholarship in school to the High School - and that he was very clever as he could easily beat him in adding up the score while playing darts in the nearby pub. He has a red-headed daughter. One girl who came on holiday to Cyffylliog was the daughter of the Lord Mayor of Liverpool, at the time. Their Liverpool accent must have rubbed off on us, because when I later went to College in Cardiff the locals thought I was a Liverpudlian. Some locals later married the evacuees. I often wonder how they coped as evacuees in more Welsh districts in rural Wales. I don't recall any serious problems with them but the local papers reported that many were lice-ridden and filthy. They were fitted up with new clothes, then went home to Liverpool within a month.

One Saturday evening I attended a call at the front door: the doctor was wanted in an emergency. He was out; so I offered to go to help, as a St John's Cadet. In a terraced house down the road an elderly man sat in an armchair, hooked by his braces in a sitting position. The wife and neighbours filled the kitchen. I did what the books say: held a mirror to his mouth and felt his pulse. As neither showed sign of life, I shook my head and told the crowd that he was dead. In anguish they all went next door for cups of tea. To check things I did the two manoeuvres again and thought I had made a mistake. There was only one thing to do - run! I called at the surgery - my home - and left a message in the call book "Mr Jones, 10 Charnel's Well - dead?"and went to the local cinema, only 100 yards away. I did not enjoy the film at all and ran home to ask my father, now in his surgery, how he found Mr Jones. "Dead, of course!" was his answer. The only time I have been glad of this diagnosis.

Before leaving school, on next to the last day, my brother climbed the school tower with our cousin Gwyn Lloyd and put a chamber pot on the top. The following day all the boys were on the school field and dared me to get Boss on to the field to see his reaction. I went to his room - had difficulty in finding a nice word for the chamber and he told me on seeing the object from the corridor to, "get the caretaker, with a long pole!" I did the same on my last day, with a pair of my father's 'long johns'. Somehow everybody knew who had done it!

CHAPTER 3

R.A.F.

I left home in September 1947, sitting on the back seat of a double decker bus. My mother had warned me about girls - 'One night with Venus, a lifetime with Mercury' - the treatment for Syphilis at that time. We waved goodbye to each other - a big lump in my throat. I had never been further than Cyffylliog on my own.

I travelled by train from Rhyl to Warrington and a bus to Padgate where we were fitted out with an RAF uniform in a week. I suppose I must have felt proud, yet jealous of my peers who had gone on to University. My brother, with the same academic problem, was an RAF Radar Engineer in Yatesbury.

After a few days in the Padgate billet the Irish Corporal who lived in a single room at the end of the 20 bedded billet, brought us all a piece of slab cake each, saying his mother had sent it as it was his birthday. After wishing him a Happy Birthday, we had the cake with a mug of tea - then had a 'whip round' for a cash gift to him. He must have done well, as we still had some cash from home. It was only about two months later when I met a Rookie who had been in the same billet and the same Irish Corporal had had a second birthday a week later and distributed slab cake from the NAAFI before a further 'whip round'!

I enjoyed the two months 'square bashing' in Bridgenorth, not too far from the Welsh border - blancoing coal and cutting the grass with our canteen knives. We were a mixed bunch, the twenty in the billet. One Cockney stood on a stool one night, told us he was illegitimate and didn't want anyone to say the word 'bastard'. I've not said it since! On another occasion, two RAF policemen came in one evening and searched my neighbour's locker. He was an older man. They found things stolen from some old lady's house down in the village nearby. He was taken away. He had tried to sell me an alarm clock a few days before but my father on the phone, advised me to reject it, "as it was probably stolen!" His First World War experiences in the trenches were apparent!

Our wages were 8 shillings a day. We would collect it on a Friday, lined up in front of the Sergeant Major at a table, march up to him, caps off and announce our RAF number (2374103 AC Thomas). Then to the NAAFI for billiards or a concert by ENSA. A pianist would be at a piano and would be given pint after pint to continue to play. There would be a sign near the billiard table, 'No walking on the table,' or shouts of, "too many balls on the table," if you lifted up a leg to reach! I learned a new language during that two months!

The training was marching, slow marching, counter marching and rifle drill all day. I enjoyed the discipline of it and the comradeship. The crude NCOs would come up close to your face and say, "Do you love me, lad?" or "Have I been in bed with your sister, lad?" They would stamp on the ground behind your feet and ask, "Am I hurting you, lad? I should be, I'm standing on your hair!"

As I said, I chose to be a nursing orderly and was sent off to Tring, near Aylesbury, in the terrible winter of 1947. I saw the New Year in sitting alone in the toilet keeping the coke fire in an oil drum stoked up to stop the pipes freezing. To celebrate, I had a meat pie and a cider. This was my first experience of alcohol, which I had been taught in Sunday School to avoid or to go to Hell.

It was known as a 'dispersed' camp, to avoid too much damage if hit by a bomb - it meant walking about a mile to the cookhouse, to enjoy hard fried eggs and bacon, or fried liver on a tray. You carried your 'irons' (cutlery) with you, with your enamel mug and plate, and washed them in boiling hot water out of doors. A Sergeant would come round at each meal and ask threateningly, "Any complaints?" I never recall a complaint! I don't remember any lessons in a classroom, only practice marching, with 40lbs on our backs in preparation for a removal to Moreton-in-the-Marsh. During one of these occasions I broke ranks as I recognised an old school friend walking along in uniform - Gwynn Llywelyn - later to become a Vetinerary Surgeon in Ruthin. We palled up and a month or so later marched from the railway station at Moreton-in-the-Marsh, the two miles to the RAF camp there. Gwynn Llywelyn was the ‘marker’ as he was 6 feet 4 inches (as are his sons now) - which meant everyone else in the troupe fell in alongside and in front of him. He would also be one of the three in front when marching, though he didn’t and doesn’t know his right from left! We had nursing classes at Moreton-in-the-Marsh and I did better than most because of my St John’s Ambulance experience. Gwynn landed me in trouble twice. He lied to a very good London boxer that I was a Welsh middle-weight champion and invited me to have a spar with him in his billet that night. I crept down and looked at him practising and I crept back to my billet. After a leg-pull· and for the sake of Wales, I returned the following evening and had a violent nose punch with blood pouring from it within a couple of minutes. Once again I returned to my billet in white (new red-stained) trunks and pumps.

On another occasion he and I went to a dance in the Town Hall. I was dancing with this strange girl when a Scottish cook tried to interrupt us. I told him to be off as she was my wife! She denied it and he said he’d see me outside. We waited for all of God Save the King and then had to leave, to be confronted by five cooks, all Glaswegians I think! I appeased the ringleader, then Gwynn Llewellyn began taking off his overcoat, as a five foot Scotsman provoked him. I told him in Welsh to keep his cool - then we both ran like hell the two miles back to camp. They were members of the Glasgow chain gang!

On another occasion one night while passing the Guard Room we were called in and told to join the RAF police in a search for a Canadian aircraftman who had broken out of the prison in the guardroom. We two tumbled out of the lorry on the Oxford Road, way out in the country, and almost held hands as we walked down the centre white line - no torches and in the dark. We heard a cough from a field on our right and could see a cigarette burning in that direction. There was nothing for it but to investigate. Looking back we deserved a DSO, or at least something. It was a sheep coughing and embers of a bonfire, not the escaped Canadian!

We went together to RAF West Kirby Hospital where, from our hut, I could see the Welsh mountains, and Moel Fammau - only twenty miles from my home but the other side of the mountain and the Dee. However, I could buy a train ticket every three months and use a platform ticket to get on to the train for my journeys home every two weeks!

Dr. J. O. Jones and William (Chauffer) on his rounds outside his Surgery.
Holywell 1918.

St. John's Cadets – Welsh First Aid winners, 1945 – Cardiff.

Sunday School Class, 1950.
Later, some became a Psychiatrist, G.P., Dental Surgeon, General Surgeon and 2 brothers are Presbyterian Ministers.

M.T.E. & D. move into Moreton in Marsh from Marsworth in March 1948.
Parade of 400 including WAAF's.
Gwyn – 'Marker' for 400 RAF marching into Moreton in Marsh 1948.
(Gwynn Llywelyn, second, right row).

Corporal Thomas – Male Nurse R.A.F.

Dr. Gwyn 1959.

Cardiff Medicals Rugby Club, 2nd fifteen.

Dr. Mari with Mrs. J. G. Thomas (author's mother)

While an 'erk' (a term used for a Private), I was punished for something I can't recall and had to brush a huge hangar full of Autumn leaves, with a small brush. I piled it all up nicely at the centre when a squad of men were marched in and through it, scattering it all again.

While in Hereford I was allowed to sleep on my own in the surgery where I was working by day. This is the time I swotted and sat an external exam successfully.

I must have felt melancholic while alone in the surgery at night. I composed the following poem about the grave:

'Lawr yn y Tywyllwch yn y bedd
Mae yna dawel - 'O hyfryd hedd -
Neb yn agos ar t wedi cau
Meddwl am hwyl yr hen ddyddiau.

Llygaid yn ddall, meddwl yn fyw
Calon yn Nefoedd - Tŷ sanctaidd Duw.
Ond beth ydyw hwn - mor llithrig i'r croen?
Pry genwar mawr - dyna ddechrau'r poen!

Bwyta ffordd trwy'r wal o bren
Dyfod yn araf ar fy mhen
Pry copyn yn cerddeg i fyny fy 'nghoes
Y mwyaf y welais yn siwr yn fy oes.

Daeth cannoedd o bryfaid, bwytasant fy nghorff
Heb gyllith na ffyrc, heb halen na thorth
'R wan mae'n nghorff yn gorwedd yn lan
Gorwedd yn lan ar pilow o groenlwch.

That is the only miserable poem that I have ever written.

"Down in the darkness in the grave
It is so quiet - 'O lovely Peace'
No one near and the roof closed
Thinking of the fun of the old days.

Eyes are blind - mind is alive
Heart in Heaven - God's holy place
But what is this - slippery to the skin?
A huge worm - here is the beginning of pain!

Eating its way through the wooden wall
Coming slowly towards my head
A spider walking up my leg
The biggest I have ever seen.

Hundreds of insects, they ate my body
Without knife or fork, without salt nor bread
Now my body is lying clean
Lying clean on a pillow of skin dust."

CHAPTER 4

Medical School

After the two years with the RAF I was admitted to the Technical College in Liverpool to do an Interim BSc course, equivalent to the Higher School Certificate again. Within a week I learned I had been accepted by Cardiff Medical School. I was delighted but a bit hurt that I was not acceptable to Liverpool Medical School, where my father and four uncles had qualified, while an aunt and mother had been in the Dental School. But it was an ill wind, as I would not have met Mari in Liverpool.

Looking for digs sounded an awesome task on the first day. We were given a list by the School Administrators but I came across another ex-Service man, Tudor Williams, from Wrexham, also looking for digs. His father was a Chest Specialist who came periodically to Denbigh Hospital and was friendly with Mr D R Edwards, who was to become founder and Chairman of Tenovus. He was the head of the Prudential Insurance for Wales.

He sent out a circular to all his agents in Cardiff to find digs for a couple of 'gogs' as we North Walians were called. We were set up with Mr and Mrs Thomas in 117 Splot Road, near the docks, where for £2.10 shillings (£2.50) each a week we had all catering except lunch on weekdays. We had single beds, a study and laundry - and it was clean! We stayed there for 2 years, often drunk after playing rugger but they proved to be a tolerant couple. We all survived. Tudor's motor bike was in the back yard. Twelve miles away in Newport lived my mother's sister, the dentist, with her family. As a treat we would motor cycle, sometimes on the pavement, to my Aunt for Sunday lunch after a couple of pints at the Tennis Club! We polished our brown boots as we sat on our beds. One night Tudor had put his heel on some polish on the lino and smeared it on his bedsheet. Despite soap it never came off. We trust that Mrs Thomas believed the truth.

I was fortunate to get the Samuel Brother's Scholarship (in Inters BSc), a £100 prize for the best student in the First Year. I had already been elected the Students' Representative and remained so for the six years. It meant I was the 'go between' in student and staff conflict. I believe I was elected this by the students because I was ex-Service and a Corporal! I had studied Physics, Chemistry and Biology once again!

At the beginning of the Second Year when we would be studying Anatomy and Physiology, we were asked to welcome the new incoming students and join them at tea. I sat next to a Mari Beddow, who appeared later that evening at the Splotland Pub, with her Howell's school friend and by now a student colleague, as I was conducting the singing from a table in the pub. That's when it all started! Her home was Cardiff; so before very long I was taken home and enjoyed many happy times with her parents in St Helen's Road, quite near the current (enormous) Heath Hospital. She was the only child, utterly spoilt by her father. He must have hated me for usurping part of his daughter Mari's affection.

My mother was often left false teeth by her deceased patients. While home on holiday once I drilled a hole in an upper set and tied a label addressed to Mari on it. Her father answered the door to the postman and was not too pleased. A typical Inland Revenue Officer!

He died suddenly after we had been courting for four years. I feel quite ashamed now that Tudor and I drove together in a Rolls Royce at his funeral at the family's expense, smiling as we drove through Cardiff. My way was now clear for Mari's mother's oxtail soup in abundance. Mari would come with us on rugger trips in the coach and to Saturday night dances in the Med Club, or down a coal mine, or a trip to Llangorse Lake with the Scientific Society. She would join in the singing and make a foursome on trips to Merthyr Mawr sand dunes.

Two years later I was awarded the Alfred Hughes Memorial Medal for Anatomy. Then came our first contact with patients on the wards, a great thrill. I recall the Professor of Medicine telling two of we men to examine the heart of a middle aged lady with pendulous breasts. I took the lead and asked my colleague on the left side of the bed to lift her left breast - he never forgave me! One lady student used to have a Petit Mal attack and drop to the floor if she laughed. We spent a lot of time 'tickling her fancy'.

During the vacation before meeting Mari I was invited to join four other ex-Service medical students, who were a year ahead of me, to tour Cornwall in two cars. We were drunk almost continually for the two weeks; we must have been because I can recall bouncing, naked, with the others into a moonlit sea with a girl from a milk bar. She was prudently covered. We slept in hedges and barns, only having a single tent for two.

While on holiday from College my brother Deri suggested a trip of ten days to Spain. We really had never been on the continent without supervision of some sort before. We borrowed mother's Austin 7 and agreed not to go more than 40 miles an hour at any time. Instead of falling out due to driving, we agreed to tap the windscreen only. We covered 3,000 miles - including a visit to Pamplona where the bulls were turned out on to the streets. An English speaker invited us to a brothel - as spectators. We agreed and sat on chairs against the wall of the glass-roofed dance hall. Soon, as Deri was trying to roll a cigarette, a girl sat next to him and offered to lick the cigarette for him, at the same time stroking his thigh. I told him - although he was two years older - to take care, in Welsh. As couples disappeared to various rooms, we left.

I must have retained some respect because I was elected the Medical School's representative on the British Medical Students' Association. This was apolitical as compared to the left wing National Union of Students. I was rung up by the Chairman for the UK (later to become Director of the NSPCC for the UK) asking if I would represent British Medical Students at a conference in Bordeaux, in France. After a chat with Mari I agreed.

As I had forgotten to put forward my watch, the loud speakers at Orly Airport blasted my name for some time before I recognised it. I landed at Bordeaux at midnight and was taken to the headquarters of the medical students and drank some frightful stuff which looked like Dettol, called Pernod. The following day, after the serious stuff, there was a banquet. A Danish student who had been to one before advised me to sit with him at the bottom of the T-shaped table. The badge of office of the French Medical Students' President was a condom stretched over a cork suspended from his neck. With each of 14 courses we were expected to take an article of clothing off. The Dane and I resisted after taking off waistcoats but others (including some of the women) were naked. Two men lay on the floor together with amorous gestures and the President - due to broadcast to the nation - was unconscious, wearing his Croix du Guerre, on the floor under the table. What a night!

Another visit to France was with the rugby team. I went as a 'Ball Boy'. We played and lost against Limoges, the pottery town, and Bergerac. We were billed as Cardiff. A banquet after each game was memorable. The wine glasses at Limoges were pottery replicas of the Captain's penis - and we had to drink out of them. In Bergerac the meal was on the village green in a marquee. On the top table were the Mayor and dignitaries. We sat in the middle table of it. Bernard, a French international, sat opposite me with his wife and challenged me to drink brandy with him. Soon my brain was gone and my bladder was full.

I presumed it was safe and micturated on the grass beneath the table. His wife shot up, soaked and shouting, "Il pissa, il pissa!". They kindly forgave me.

Rag Week was a week of extra revelry. We would parade through the city on the back of lorries with students of the other faculties, to raise cash for local charities. A Rag Magazine was published and often uncensored. We took extra liberties and a blind eye was taken by the Police and College Authorities that week.

For a few weeks, to save on the price of cinemas and to learn of other cultures, Mari and I toured various religious bases - Christian Scientist, Seven-day Adventists, Roman Catholic and others. At one, we sat in a circle and a lady went into a trance. She then went on the outside of the circle and put her hands on each person's shoulder and made some comment, for instance, a message from a deceased relative. It was just before one of my final exams. As she laid her hands on my shoulder she said, much to my delight, "Christ's Spirit of healing is radiating from you!" Mari was told, "God bless you my child." (She never failed an exam!). I must have been stinking of Dettol!

Most Saturday nights dances, to a band of three, would be held in the front room of the converted house in Howard Gardens, Cardiff -it was our Medical Club. I don't recall a bar there but the Splotlands Pub was only a few yards away. Occasionally a Fancy Dress Dance would be held there. Mari and I won it twice, once as

'Bill and Ben, the Flowerpot Men' and another time as 'the two old ladies who lived in a lavatory'. We were both dressed as old ladies and the design, in material of a lavatory seat, was stitched, half on each of the back of our dresses. Mr Dodsworth, the Medical School Secretary, popped in to make sure all was well. We would eat our meals there, four times a day if resident. At lunch time the Consultants and Professors would have their own table.

Cliff, the Dissecting Room Technician, invited Mari and myself to tea in a council house in Ely, which was very nice of him. Professor 'Pop' Watkins had us for Sunday tea; then the Senior Anatomist invited us both to his house for supper. It was rather daunting. He was from Liverpool, and his wife a Venereologist. As we two sat at the fireside she asked Mari which school she went to, (She replied, "Howell's, Cardiff.") then if she had any siblings - she denied any. To this Mrs Hughes said, "You must be a spoilt snob." Mari had, in fact, won a scholarship to the school. Dr Hughes, to make me feel at home, asked if if I had read much of Chaucer. I had not read a thing of the man. He then proceeded to read The Miller's Tale to me. I enjoyed only the naughty bits! As House Doctors, we were also invited to Mari's Surgical boss's house, a wealthy steel works family in Cardiff. The only thing I recall is a duck being brought in on a silver salver with a lid to it!

Mr Hector Thomas and his hockey-playing (for Wales) wife Enid would hold jolly parties for the whole First XV and others while the teams held annual dinners, in the cellar of the Queen's Hotel, when Mr Cecil Lewis (later Professor in Perth, Australia) would play the piano for rugger songs and survive pints of beer being poured over him as he played.

We worked and played hard at the Medical School. I became the Business Manager of 'The Leech', our annual journal. I understood from the College Secretary that it was the first time it had shown a profit. I took advantage of this post to get into a miners' rally in Cory Hall in Cardiff, to see and hear Aneurin Bevan. I noticed a doctor member of the Pathology Department come into the crowded hall carrying a thick medical text book and wearing a polo neck pullover. As Bevan stated that he wanted to quantify the amount of illness amongst miners by looking at the Death Certificates, the Pathologist kept saying "Rubbish" from the back of the hall. Aneurin Bevan finally stopped and repeated that he was talking about gross figures and did not expect to see the exhibition of gross bad manners from the "back of the 'all". Put him in his place! On another occasion I climbed up a ladder to the roof of the entrance at the City Hall, to be near Winston Churchill - 10 yards away - as he made a public speech to the crowd below.

As the Cardiff representative of the British Medical Students' Association I was appointed the Chairman of the Association for Oxford, Birmingham, Bristol and Cardiff Medical Schools following the now Dr John Hughes, Aberystyth and as such had to represent them at a meeting at Whitley Bay, taking a student friend, David Millward, with me. A meeting at Oxford was hilarious. We had a crate of beer on the boardroom table and a chamber pot under it. I have a photograph of an Oxford student, later to become Regional Adviser in General Practice in Scotland, carrying the pot to be emptied!

Another high spot was being made Chairman of the 'Med. Pres. Ball' Committee, an important annual ball held in the City Hall, the Castle, or the Drill Hall. I felt peeved that the Medical School staff had to have a private bar and restaurant and did not mix with the students. A Staff President was elected each year. One of my Committee arranged the catering and got a big 'back hander' for it. He later worked in Harley Street!

I was Captain of the Thirds in my second year, never having seen rugger before going to Cardiff, then was promoted to the Seconds because I could lead the singing on the coaches. We would travel to the Valley teams and played the Westminster Hospital in London. We slept in the gymnasium there. I recall David Williams, who had only one leg, climbing up a rope and sleeping on one of the beams. Another boy, naked, pinched a bike and cycled through the Nurses' Home, oblivious to their loud screams. He became an Eye Specialist in Cardiff. Full of beer, we stood on the bottom step of the bus and urinated as the bus drove through the night, passing bus queues on one occasion!

After one Saturday match a gang of us went to Splot to Sam on Yen's for supper. I was asked to check the kitchen and reported that Sam was cutting up a chicken with his hands. A row broke out and the Police were called. The Sergeant recognised us as the team they had played that afternoon and settled all amicably.

It was at this time that when home on vacation I went with my father to see an elderly farmer, in his bedroom, with prostate trouble. He was turned on to his left side. My father put some soap under his right index finger nail - deformed since a bullet in the trenches - and put it up the farmer's back passage, to test the gland. He then turned to me and asked if I had learned to do this. I proudly said yes - then he told me to do the same, which I refused without a rubber finger stall. He hesitantly produced one from his waistcoat pocket. I did the examination and was about to tear the rubber off to discard, when he stopped me and told me to wash it in the cold water in the pot jug and basin in the bedroom. Then he dried it on the bedclothes and put it back in his pocket!

The sessions dissecting the bodies, pickled in formalin, were social occasions. Our cigarettes would be soaked in formaldehyde but we cared nothing.

Although having had three prizes in the Medical School in Inter BSc, Anatomy and Paediatrics, I failed the last medical exam. I felt now I knew all the rare things but not the more common things like treating heart failure. I then spent six months in free digs in Whitchurch Hospital on condition that I did a quick ward round once a night.

I had had some odd digs in the city beforehand. In one, a spinster just gave me shop fish and chips, then a banana for an evening meal nightly and she kept warm sitting by an open oven! This was in a posh part of Cardiff.

I was proud to be asked by the Professor of Child Health to be Father Christmas at the Cardiff Royal Infirmary Staff Children's Christmas Party in the Outpatients' Department.

At Christmas the Medical and Physiotherapy students got together to produce a pantomime, which was to run for four days in the Outpatients' Hall. We had a lot of fun preparing this. Apart from the pantomime there would be short sketches. Mari took part in one - I was taking the role of the Professor of Surgery Lambert Rogers in the pantomime, about a mock love affair with a Nursing Sister. I had a lot of solo singing to do. The annual event was called "The Anencephalics', which means born without a brain. A Consultant Dermatologist checked the script and refused to allow a song to be sung, written about a male nurse named Basil - "I'm Basil from Cory, Mametz and Glan Ely. I'm very fond of the lads. Wouldn't it feel good in bed with John Guilgud, as sodomy's one of my fads!" This was disallowed. Cory, Mametz and Glan Ely were names of the wards and he was a homosexual.

Because of my North Walian accent and loud voice, for two

successive years I was asked to announce the Proclamation of the Medical School Degree Ceremony - "Gorau awen Gwirionedd, Bydded hysbys i Llys etc." It was quite an honour. I didn't know who did it when in1956 I had my medical degree presented to me. In fact, I don't recall the moment! Mari qualified six months later, – not presumably because of the pantomime role!

My first job as a doctor was as a House Surgeon to the famous Professor Lambert Rogers, an ex-Naval Australian. We had to parade in front of him each morning, report on the number of empty beds on his ward and what had been admitted during the night. There were so many senior to me that I did very little surgery but wrote up the histories. We did ward rounds with him and his second in command, who was very religious, but I felt he had no warmth towards the patients. The Professor's only child was brought to the Casualty Department when I was on duty, as a student, and I sutured her cut head. That is how I got the job on his firm later – not presumably because of the Pantomime role!

I applied for, and obtained, a six month appointment as Obstetric House Surgeon to Professor Duncan. This was in a new building opposite the Royal Infirmary. It was a busy job as one attended all the deliveries for their firm. Unfortunately the Professor had a coronary thrombosis while I was attached to his firm, which gave greater responsibility to his juniors. I can recall a woman choking while being induced by an anaesthetist. He panicked while the more senior obstetrician and I were preparing to do the Caesarean operation on her. We stood each side of her head and the Senior Registrar cut open her throat, told me to tie off the bleeding parts there and he made a hole in her windpipe to allow her to breathe again. The neck was then tidied up by the Ear, Nose and Throat staff, while we got on with the Caesarean successfully with a different anaesthetist.

It may have been on the strength of this experience that I was asked to be present at the birth of the Jewish Obstetrician's first baby and later invited to the circumcision ceremony. I had to wear a bowler hat and stood in a small group of about 8 men watching and celebrating after. I was so moved by it that I wrote a small poem:-

Caethom gip ar cock rhyw grwtyn
Yn disgyn o'i gafael cul
Wen ar wyneb wen y gwendid
Gaed a gwin rhed ar yr wyl.

"We had a look at a small creature's penis -
Bit falling off its narrow end
A smile on the pale face of the injured
Blood and wine flowed at the Ceremony."

The father was later to become a Consultant Obstetrician in Newport, Monmouthshire.

I then did six months enjoyable Paediatrics in Church Village Hospital, near Pontypridd, later in Practice to obtain an examination and Diploma in Child Health. I would pop to Cardiff, in a car my father had given me, to see Mari as often as I could. Then I had a job as a Senior House Officer in Medicine, in the Abergavenny Hospital, by the order of Professor Scarborough (Medicine). To my joy I was invited to fish the River Wye there and to the Golf Club. At that time Mari was in Wrexham Maelor Hospital. I had found that people were dying and being taken off to the mortuary, without a doctor seeing them. I changed this. One dawn I was called to see an old lady who had died in a double room; she was near the window and behind a screen. An Italian sat next to his ill wife on the other side. As I examined the old lady I saw a fat pigeon on a branch of a fir tree nearby. I returned with my shotgun, purchased as a student from none other than the now renowned Forensic Professor Sir Bernard Knight, which I had hidden under my white coat. I took a pot shot at the pigeon and missed it. The old lady was soon wheeled out of the ward covered by a sheet, to the horror of the Italian, who discharged his wife the following day - he hadn't agreed to euthanasia!

After seven years' courtship I asked Mari to marry me, in the bathroom of her home in Cardiff. She agreed! We married on 15 February 1958 at North Road, Cardiff. We had not been allowed to use the unconsecrated hospital chapel, though we had wedding presents and attendance by Professor Lambert Rogers and Mari's surgical chief. Mari's father had died three years before. I'm not quite sure if he would have approved, as I used to put my feet on his mantlepiece as he and I both watched TV. My father did not attend. He had not turned up in Hull for Deri's wedding either but he did turn up at Gwenllian's at our local chapel and reception. However, as he'd had a stroke by this time he had no option. He had not attended our graduations either. My mother was pleased to make a speech in all the weddings.

Mari didn't know where I had planned the honeymoon - the Scilly Isles - but I had told my father. He told me that a girl from Llansannan had gone somewhere there. As we left the hotel the chambermaid told me that she was the one!

CHAPTER 5

General Practice

Midwifery and Suicides

We came North, in March 1958, for me to work with my father and his partner and purchased a semi-detached house in the town. For the earlier years it was difficult. The appointment system had not started and if my father saw someone in the waiting room when I was home having a meal, he would 'phone for me to come at once to see the patient. He received double the partner's salary, which he split with me. He could then say that, if the partner complained that he was not doing his share, I was being paid to do it! He had done his share over 35 years, most of it on his own with, at that time, 2000 patients covering 300 square miles.

This partner, a strange choice for my father who was so Welsh, was his second partner. The first, from North Wales, had gone to bed in our home early one night, when I was home on leave from the RAF, and I noticed his uneaten supper in the oven. I went up to his bedroom to ask if he wanted to eat it or not. Through indirect light I saw him lying on the bedroom floor in his pyjama trousers, masked and his feet and hands tied. At first I thought a burglar had done it, then understood. I undid his hands and he saw to the rest saying, "Silly thing to do," repeatedly. He was obviously a masochist. I realised then what he used to do when going for a walk at night with a small leather case!

At the very first I had to use the dispensary as a consulting room. There were only we three doctors; no staff in those days. We would have to count the tablets and mix the medicines - one ounce of concentrated medicine from a Winchester bottle then filled with seven ounces of water. The usual medicines were for a cough - one if productive, different if dry, a mixture for cystitis, to increase appetite and gallons of white medicine dispensed for dyspepsia, which was much more common in those days. Until about 1946 water was carried in an enamel jug from the cellar kitchen to make the medicines. Heat and light was, as I said, by gas and paraffin.

In the first week I was taking a history from a woman who complained that her husband's urine hurt her leg! My father was standing behind her smiling. I had not spotted that the poor lady was a schizophrenic and hallucinating!

My father retired after we had worked together for two or three years, leaving me with the rather shy, withdrawn man, who lived very close by. We worked together for about ten years; then suddenly he did not turn up. His wife took his name off his consulting room door and put it up in a house 100 yards away. The poor man only lived two years and she lived another couple.

Mari, having worked in Child Clinics and Psychiatry at the North Wales Hospital, then had a seven year gap to bring up the three adopted children. She joined me after I had worked alone and happily for ten years or so. They were now very busy and happy years as the practice expanded. She took so long to get dressed and made up for her first night call, I told her not to bother again and I went - until the last night she was in general practice when she did one!

In the meantime, I had taken on a partner who remained there until I retired; now the firm has five excellent doctors and a trainee GP. We had one receptionist in 1962, and a staff of at least ten when I left. Mrs Carys Jones started as a receptionist over 30 years ago and is still there. She and Mari were the backbone of all the things I did. She used to come with her two little daughters during their primary school holidays. They are both mothers now!

It was during the three years that my father worked with us that a farmer from the depths of the Denbigh Moors called to the surgery and mentioned that his 11 year old daughter couldn't stand. He was given the inevitable Aspirin and told to report in the morning. She was no better. It had snowed a great deal in the night. I drove as near to the farm as I could and walked through the blizzard the remaining mile. I must admit that I thought she was being hysterical, as her legs collapsed beneath her. She said she had Polio. "How ridiculous!" I thought. To avoid another visit I put her in her father's car and dragged it with the tractor to my car.

While at the surgery and trying to find a bed for her, she coughed. I now realised this was real. She was in an iron lung that evening, with Poliomyelitis. Many years later, she was one of my daughter's teachers; she had already taught me a lesson.

During that period I was called to the bungalow of a friend of the family where the young father of 40 years had what sounded like indigestion. While I was listening to his heart, in the bedroom, it stopped. I failed to get it restarted and had to go out to face the young family to explain that it was a thrombosis after all and that he was dead. I believe that episode was one of the worst I was to experience. Many years later I had what I felt was the worst testing day of my career. Two families, patients of mine, had each lost a teenage child, boy and girl sweethearts, in the Manchester Air Disaster. I visited both families that day to try to help, but helplessly. Then I visited a third family who had escaped. The contrast was awful, as the TV cameras were at the third home, amongst much jubilation.

I was not happy for another reason, when I was called to a home near Llanefydd. Again, I had to walk from bed through snow at midnight. The elderly lady, not very bright, wanted something for her painful corn!

On another snowy occasion, I was called to a small farmhouse near the top of the Clwydian Range in the early evening. The grandfather had not got out of bed, so the household was concerned. I had to climb over the snow covered hedges to get to the house. The nice old boy in bed asked what I wanted and he said his watch had stopped so he didn't know what the time was! A silent swear and I felt better! One other occasion, near Nantglyn, I had to climb over snow to the middle-aged lady with bronchitis. I was alarmed and upset that I had forgotten my stethoscope, so got her to sit up, lean forward and take some breaths as I held the bottom of a small bottle over her back lungs, unknown to her. She was none the worse.

Before my father retired he told me to apply for a paid Clinical Assistantship which was advertised every three years, for a half-day operating surgery at the Infirmary. I managed to take it from another practice which already had two Clinical Assistantships; so justice was done. I bet my father was pleased, as they had been old rivals. He did not comment to me. This meant that I had Monday afternoons for the next 35 years to do minor operations at the

Denbighshire Infirmary and was paid for it. I treated varicose veins, hydroceles, sebacious cysts, abscesses and even cosmetic surgery once, when I cut off bags under a middle-aged lady's eyes. With Mr Robert Owen, later to become as I have said, Professor of Orthopaedics at Liverpool, we amputated a postman's leg under a general anaesthetic given by Dr Frost: the last major operation carried out at the Infirmary.

After a few years I was undertaking more minor operations on my half-day than a colleague from another practice was doing in a paid whole day and, at a doctors' meeting, I suggested that it was only fair that we now swap, with the ensuing double in salary. The colleague was twenty years my senior and was so shocked by my suggestion that he hit me on the chest with his fist.

During a Parliamentary Election, I was walking down a footpath to a house in Groes, carrying my bag, to be met by the Labour Candidate, Mrs Ann Clwyd, whose uncle was a GP in Denbigh. She didn't know me, particularly as the President of the Liberals in Denbigh, and told me of her politics and asked would I vote for her. She recognised my doctor's bag; then I offered her a baby from it and I told her that I was on my way to Llansannan Surgery and would see her in the local pub there later. I had never drunk in a 'local' in the village. We didn't meet - but the following Tuesday I crept into the packed hall to listen to the Labourites. She was speaking, saw me at the back door and obviously had, in the meantime, found out who I was and said to the crowd, "Dr Gwyn Thomas has obviously finished his pint and come here to listen!" It floored me. Her GP uncle was on the stage with her. She failed to get into Parliament until she tried in the South Wales Valleys.

The Liberal Candidate, during a visit to my home, was asked by local Alderman Hywel Owen if he had ever seen the ghost near the Brenig River (now the Reservoir) on the Moors. It was 11.30 at night. Hywel had seen it often and offered to take us both there to see it. He made us both stand in the river, in wellingtons, at midnight and wait - while he sat in the dry, warm car. We stood there - real 'Charlies', for half an hour and saw nothing but a smile on Hywel's face! The Parliamentary Candidate was a GP from Southport and used to impress me, in 1966, by having the first mobile phone I had seen - in his Rolls Royce! the car a gift, I believe, from a patient.

I kept a little note in my wallet for years, from a lady on the Council Estate which said, "Can I have another bottle of the cough mixture, the one that makes my husband hurry when we are having intercourse!" - badly spelt.

Then another problem was an obese girl of 30 who complained that her husband was unable to perform (he was probably too drunk). I advised her to go out to the country to a field, for a change. Later she said that they tried in the back of the car but had forgotten to put on the brake and the car rolled down the field.

One lady reminded Mari recently that as she worked in a launderette opposite my surgery window. I would 'phone her to put her cigarette out as she tried to have a quiet whiff at work! Her brother had died young from a coronary thrombosis. Later, she had one and survived.

I took part in the delivery of a total of 1,500 babies, most at Denbighshire Infirmary where about 2000 deliveries took place annually About 2,500 were being delivered in the.Consultant Unit at St Asaph under Mr Parry Jones and Mr Holmes. At first we could take on any potential mother, dependent on their wishes. They were kept in for two weeks if it was the first baby, or ten days if not and there were no complications. It gave the mother a rest and a chance to have constant help with the baby. After about 20 years, the Peel Report was published with the advice that only the second baby and onwards should be delivered at home or in GP beds. It saved a lot, but not all, of my sweating with anxiety.

I had come from a Professor's Obstetric Unit as a House Surgeon and later, from Practice, passed exams for a Diploma in Obstetrics - but in spite of this Sister Jones, a very well-known Sister in charge of the Unit in Denbigh, treated all the doctors as students! I had asked for a mask, cap, gown and wellingtons, to do a forceps delivery, as I had been trained, to be told to do without and "bloody get on with it!" with a cigarette or pipe in her mouth. She was really great and, as far as I knew, no problem arose, even in the 'loneliest place in the world', one's hand in the woman's uterus feeling and peeling away any bits of placenta left inside, with the danger of bleeding as you took your hand out before giving the injection into a vein to clamp down the womb.

There was a Flying Squad based at St Asaph, if one got into trouble. The only time I needed one was when the skin of the vagina was like a dry washleather with a tear in it. Each time I tied a knot in it another appeared - so did the blood. In desperation I rang the sole Obstetrician and he told me to push a hot wet towel into the vagina for quarter of an hour. I did this and to my delight, as I removed the towel, the bleeding had stopped. There was nothing sweeter than hearing the baby cry as you walked down the corridor to the labour ward - cared for by the midwife.

On one occasion I had a lady in labour there and another in Brynrhydyrarian in the evening. I thought the latter would come first, on the observations of the district midwife. I got to the cottage nine miles away, to find that it was in early stages and didn't have enough petrol to come back, so sat in the kitchen upright chair for hours knowing that Sister Jones would see the other lady safe. It all went well: we never lost a baby or mum.

One Sunday morning a lady was in labour in the Infirmary and progress came to a halt. I rang the Consultant; this one was from Wrexham. He asked me to fix up an Anaesthetist (a lady doctor from Ruthin) and he would come over to do a Caesarean section with me. The Anaesthetist told me she couldn't come, as she was preparing Sunday dinner for her family. On reporting this to the Obstetrician he said, "You'll have to give the anaesthetic, Gwyn." I really had minimal experience of anaesthetics, even dental ones but, as a boy, I had watched my father give chloroform and ether, dropping the mixture from a bottle on to a mask on the patient's face. I put her under using this; then she started vomiting. I sucked the throat clean with a crude sucker from the water tap nearby and kept going. A lovely baby girl was delivered. Mother was stitched up and she started vomiting again. I asked Sister Jones whether the patient had had breakfast. She replied, "She had a lovely breakfast." God is good!

I am reminded of a time when I was on a farm at Bodfari seeing to a man with a dangerous pulmonary embolus following an operation, in Liverpool, on his knee. I had to get him to the Royal Alexandra Hospital at that time. The switchboard in Denbigh was manually operated by a Mr Williams. On offering the telephone number he recognised my voice and told me my wife and mother were looking for me for an emergency. I left the farmer and I recall revving the engine of my new car over the red mark to get to Love Lane in Denbigh where a woman, a newcomer to the town, was having a fit on the kitchen floor. An eclamptic fit - I'd never seen one before. A baby was due in a week. I injected various sedatives into her veins, to no avail. Finally I soaked the kitchen towel with a type of chloroform and put her to sleep, keeping her like this in the ambulance until she delivered, by section, the live baby in St Asaph. The farmer in Bodfari did well, to become the "World Champion Ploughman"!

I was phoned at two in the morning on one occasion as a farmer's wife, six miles away, told me on the phone that her 20 year old single daughter had colic two hours before and she had given her liquid paraffin, only to hear a baby crying in the bed now! I picked up the district midwife and tidied up the young mother and the delightful, unexpected baby.

A very religious unorthodox lady, living in a flat in the town, started off in labour in her home as she had demanded - her first pregnancy! The midwife checked her periodically while I sat in the kitchen, as I was not allowed to see her 'private parts', as it said in the Bible! The pains stopped; so I was pleased that I could now send her into hospital. The couple refused and prayed for ten minutes, when the pains returned. She delivered a lovely boy with the biggest baby penis I'd ever seen. She said she was grateful to me and would like to use my first name, John - omitting my surname - for the baby! I agreed. Now the problem was she had torn her 'tail' and it needed stitching. No way could I stitch it blindfold but she was so delighted when I put the baby to her breast that she didn't notice my putting in the stitches at her lower end.

When someone was in labour in the Infirmary while I was ten miles away, in my branch surgery at Llansannan on a Tuesday night, I would periodically walk to the telephone kiosk 100 yards away and check with the Labour Ward. As soon as I heard, "Fully dilated!" I would leave the surgery temporarily and get down to the Labour Ward in 12 minutes. The roads were quieter then. My father had had the tradition of attending every labour, even though normal. I think it was because you'd be paid more by the Executive Council for the service.

An abortionist used to live in the council houses in Denbigh. She would introduce a needle to the uterus and rid one of the unwanted pregnancies. She was a big, strong woman and although what she was doing was a criminal offence, no one reported her. There was always the danger of infection, bleeding, or ruptured uterus. I found that once the foetal movements were felt by the girl, at 18 weeks of pregnancy, the girls kept the baby. This was before the 'pill'. I was aware that my father would give abortifacient tablets - Penny Royal, iron, or quinine bark into the neck of the womb to stimulate contractions but I never took the chance. Families were big in those days. My father delivered 15 babies to one lady - most survived and are about now, including the mother.

One could do very little for infertility, in those carly days, though I was able to cure two women. One complained that the pet dog jumped on to the bed when she and her husband 'made love'. Keeping a straight face, I advised her to close the door on the dog. She later adopted her children. Another had been trying for a baby for three years. I examined her and was surprised to see that she was still a virgin. They were not the brightest - though from a rural community. He'd been using the wrong orifice all the time. I advised her and she conceived that night. Now she has two grown-up children.

I was, of course, particularly sympathetic to patients with infertility problems. When I retired I had two couples who had waited two years for a baby to be available for adoption. I would telephone the County Council Adoption Officer and the relevant local County Councillor for help. There were, at that time, only ten babies a year for adoption in the County (population 300,000) and mothers were given the choice of what sort of home to which they would like their baby to go. More often than not it would be to very young couples - the same age group as themselves,which eliminated older couples who had been waiting a while. Husbands over 40 years of age were eliminated anyway.

When the wife of an infertile couple had been examined and perhaps reassured by the gynaecologist, it would be the turn of the husband to be examined, though really it was much easier to exclude any problems with him first. A sperm count would be necessary, assuming the physical examination was normal. The specimen had to be received in the hospital laboratory within a couple of hours. Because patients, usually farmers, lived far from the Royal Alexandra Hospital, I would tell them to take the little bottle and disappear into the sand dunes opposite the hospital in Rhyl - with or without his wife - and to try to keep one eye open lest the police should interfere. I would somehow give the orders seriously yet lightheartedly, so the patient would not be too embarrassed - nor me! There were no police helicopters in those days.

In my early days it was the responsibility of the man who had fathered an illegitimate birth to pay 7/6d (approximately 40p) a week to the mother. Two men met while walking down the path to a cottage in Groes and admitted to each other that they were, and had been, paying 7/6d a week to the same girl for the same baby. She was an entrepreneur!

As a rural practitioner one sees and hears odd things. In my early days, an eighteen year old Welsh speaking farm labourer came and complained that the flies talked to him as he had breakfast. Then he admitted that the birds talked to him about the soil. He admitted that he was fond of animals - even loved the pigs on the farm. When I asked him if he ever showed his love for the pigs, he admitted he did. I, shocked, asked him which he used, the pigs or the sows: he answered in disgust, "the sows, of course - there's nothing wrong with me!" Today, I would probably have a chat with him. In those days I admitted him to the North Wales Mental Hospital for six months. When discharged I asked him how he had started the bestiality. He admitted to using hens. There is much talk of the Welsh and sheep. I never came across it. A cow - yes.

About two years after starting in practice I thought it could be useful to get a further diploma. This was to be in Child Health -as I had won the Year's Prize in the subject as a student. It was difficult to find time to swot. Then I had to go to London to sit the exam and the practicals. While waiting in Great Ormond Street Hospital, for my practical exam, I went to look for an old pal, then a Professor of Paediatrics and found him lecturing, as I peered through a porthole in the door of the lecture theatre. He was addressing a sea of faces of all colours when he spotted me. He called me in, took my overcoat off and told the crowd of students "Dr Gwyn Thomas had come all the way from North Wales to tell us how he would do a tracheotomy (making a hole in the windpipe) on a newborn baby in North Wales!" Taken aback, I replied, "I'd hold the head back, cut a hole in the pipe and stick a hollow bit of straw in it!" I swore I'd get my own back one day.

A 25 year old good-looking lady, a stranger, came into my room one day and sat down. I greeted her cheerfully and told her to put her feet on my desk while I went to collect some papers. When I returned, she had her feet on my desk! I soon realised that she had come into town from the North Wales Mental Hospital, which was up the road, not an uncommon practice. I dealt with her and off she went. A little while later I was on the High Street walking to the shops on a busy market day. She saw me and shouted from the other side of the crowded road, "Are you still playing with yourself, Dr Gwyn?"

I had a lot of night calls, most of them worthwhile, though in the very early days I was called to a Council home in town at 2 o'clock. I found the kitchen full of family and neighbours and the 18 year old lying on the floor drunk, refusing to go to bed for his equally drunk mother. As I entered she shouted to the boy, "You'll have to go to bed now, Dr Gwyn is here!" He opened his eyes, looked at me and said, "F... off!" which I did! Most of the night calls were people having a heart attack or asthma. I don't recall having to send any asthmatic to hospital. Inhalers and reassurance were all that was needed, though I do recall sending a woman in - she was black in the face - on whom I had had to do a mouth-to-mouth resuscitation. This, again, was in the early days.

I was called to my mother five times for heart failure attacks, usually at 5 or 6 in the morning. Intravenous injection and oxygen put things right until the last time, when I was away.

I suppose many people were grateful for what I tried to do. It was in the days when Bank Managers, Ministers and local Politicians had some priority in the surgeries. Pre-National Health, Ministers were not charged. I'm not sure of the others. I remember inheriting part of this convention. The Bank Manager's wife would sit in my mother's sitting room and I would have to go to collect her to take her to my consulting room. It grieved me a bit, this scheme of things. However, her elderly husband died and she invited me to her home to show me her appreciation. With some anxiety on my part she invited me upstairs into a small box room, and gave me his size 6 top hat (I am 7 !), a yellowing silk scarf and a nice pullover. I had spotted two old fishing rods in the corner. I asked to see them and then she asked me how much I thought they were worth. I suggested £5 each. She asked if I would like them. To which I said I'd be delighted. She charged me all I'd got in my pocket - £9.10s!

I used to give lectures, as a 16 yr. old to Trefnant Youth Club - later, as a doctor, to the local St John's Ambulance Brigade and examine the competitors in the National Eisteddfod when teams of Police or Coal Miners, from Wrexham and South Wales, would compete.

It was possibly this which helped me almost to enjoy accidents in the fields or on the road. Often I would take charge of the incident. I recall tractor accidents, one near Peniel, when the farmer was trapped under his tractor over a stream for four hours. When I asked him what he did all that time, he said pray that his wife would come with his tea and find him. The big wheel had to be taken off to release him - with minor injuries. Another time, 15 miles away the farmer was under a tractor with crushed ribs, and it was down a steep field. We put him on two planks across the back of a four-wheeled pick-up, to get him to the ambulance.

Another tractor overturned in Nantglyn, rupturing the young farmer's spleen. He crawled to the road. I was there before the ambulance. He did all right. A young, rather wild, contractor overturned his caterpillar tractor while ploughing heather and gorse on top of a very steep hillock. My son Rhys, aged 15 then, was with me and he carried my bag to the overturned machine. The man had fractured his pelvis. The ambulance and police arrived as we lowered him on a corrugated iron sheet, controlled by a rope, down the very steep slope to the ambulance. He did well.

The only tractor accident, with a sad ending, was when a patient of mine drove his tractor in the field with a loaded shotgun on it. It fell off, went off and killed him.

I did a fair amount of shooting until recently, beating a farmer's hedge, with my Springer spaniel. Robert Owen would come with me in the winter and we had good exercise chasing pheasants and rabbits. I only once paid for a season's shoot near Flint. I can't say I enjoyed the flock of pheasants coming over me and shooting them. I enjoyed the picnic with the beaters but not too much with the Cheshire set. I don't think I was too welcome as I 'shot low'. Having smashed the head of my left upper arm, on the ice of Austria some years before, I found it difficult to shoot high. Fox shooting, with a syndicate, is exciting. I shot one fox as it came towards me on the other side of a fence as beaters drove it. Another I shot by my front door as it chewed laurel fruit. I have no hesitation in killing them. One got five of my hens, a beautiful cockerel and two ducks in one episode.

I saw a man, when I was 15 years old, who had shot off the top of his head, as his wife had incorrectly thought he had been unfaithful. Then on another occasion, while dressing for the Rotary Ball at the North Wales Hospital, I had a message from a gardener five miles away to visit the roadway outside the patient's home. I rushed there - bow tie and all - to find the man with the shotgun still in his hands. He had given his wife a bunch of flowers, as it was her birthday the following day, then gone outside and done that! I had to go to the wife to tell her what had happened. I suppose he was only one of perhaps three of my patients who had committed suicide but nonc had been on treatment. My wife says those on treatment were too scared of me to try! A famous Welsh Consultant Psychiatrist, in 1960, asked me to do a survey on my patients, on the incidence of neurosis in my typical North Wales practice, as he wanted to do a survey in Anglesey for his MD thesis. One in three had had some sort of neurosis - the same as he found in Anglesey.

I recall a farmer whose two brothers had hanged themselves in my father's time. I was expecting the next brother to present himself one day. He arrived, complaining that he had, "lost his look forward" - half in Welsh and half in English, a beautiful description of depression in the early stages. I had heard the cuckoo the previous evening while fishing up on the moors. I told him to go and listen that night, knowing that most country people enjoy the sound. He returned the following day much better - but I also gave him some antidepressant tablets, just in case! He lived many years.

When patients were in the process of being discharged, to empty the Mental Hospital as far as possible, a number went to a hostel near Wrexham, which was soon condemned. These people were transferred to Grove Hall, Bodfari, under the care of Mrs Edith Jones. It proved a tremendous success. About 100 ex-patients lived in a community enjoying the freedom of the countryside and each other's company. Later, when Llangwyfan Hospital closed it was taken over by the ex-Deputy Director of Social Services as a private home for youngsters with some mental problems. In all, we had 250 patients classed as problematical nervous disorder patients, in the practice, a ratio probably more per doctor than anywhere in the country. There was never any serious problem with any of them. Recently the practice gained the National Award for the care of Schizophrenics.

One of my most famous patients was a pretty, sad lady who lived alone. She wrote historical stories and sad novels. Her brother had died in the Mental Hospital.

She was one of our most difficult patients - though grateful as she realised the problems she gave. She is the only patient about whom I heard my father complain. She fell one Sunday morning, and neighbours had spotted that she had not taken in her milk. I was sent for and found her upstairs with a fractured arm. I made her comfortable, wrapped her in a blanket, and sent for an ambulance. She then said she wanted to use the toilet. I made the mistake of going in first, to the small toilet, and was trapped as she insisted that I undress her! She must have been a record for her age! After she was in the Infirmary for six months with various life endangering conditions, she went home to her house to live alone, in her late 80s.

I would enjoy my Monday afternoon minor operating session. One of the earliest operations was unsuccessfully stitching back two fingers on a girl who had cut them off with a lawn mower. She is now a nursing sister. Microsurgery was in its infancy in the major hospitals, let alone the local Infirmary.

One day a 30 year old local man came to me complaining that his penis was too small and that, as he walked into a pub, the people would point at him and comment on this fact. Poor man was a paranoid depressive who needed hospital treatment lest he killed himself. He refused admission to our local huge mental hospital, as the staff would recognise him. I admitted him to Chester Mental Hospital - a thing I had never done before or after. He was discharged the following day as he was caught in bed that night with a female patient! I lost contact with the man.

In my early years I was invited to talk to the Nantglyn Young Farmers' Club and I chose the subject 'Having a baby', going to a lot of trouble to prepare a talk with slides. At the end of the talk a young man stood to thank me and said that they were more interested in stopping having babies than having them!

CHAPTER 6

General Practice

Committees and Cases

Once a month, on Sundays, the Clwyd Local Medical Committee would meet. We were voted onto it, to represent the General Practices of Clwyd County. Ours was a very influential Committee nationally, thanks to the likes of the late Dr David Williams of Holywell and Dr John Lynch OBE of Denbigh - both to become very senior members of the BMA in London, the latter unfortunately to suffer a stroke while at a London meeting. Then Dr Eddie Lewis, of Mold, followed the late Dr Ivor Davies of Cerrigydruidion, as the efficient Secretary. At present, he is Provost of the North Wales Faculty of the Royal College of General Practitioners, which I founded in 1987.

I had been Chairman of the Clwyd Local Medical Committee for three years. We dealt with administrative aspects of GP medicine. The Local Medical Committee elected three of its members to the Disciplinary Committee of the Family Health Services Committee, a most important sub-committee of the FHSA, where doctors were examined in a pseudo-Court situation. A defence was arranged and a prosecution. Lay people presided. I was one of the 'jury' of three GPs. It proved most interesting, though for a short time the same GP kept appearing following complaints by relations, many of whom felt guilty after the loss of a relation whom they had not visited for some time. The Chief Executive of the FHSA was Major-General Chris Last, a most formidable, intelligent, informed Chief of the Dental, Pharmaceutical and General Practice Services. He had picked up the job very quickly, following on from the sympathetic Mrs Jackson and the more uncooperative

Mr Tunnah whom, we felt, was influenced by the late Dr Choudhry, a local politician of great experience. Mr Tom Jones, now Chairman of Flintshire County Council, was its very humane Chairman.

About this time, I had been Treasurer of the North Wales Branch of the BMA for a few years and on its North Clwyd Executive. I was elected Chairman of the Executive for three years. About the same time I was elected Chairman of the Clwyd District Medical Committee - a post alternating with a three year rotation with hospital consultants. I followed the late Dr Bob Jones of Rhyl, a well-known GP. We would meet in the Health Authority Headquarters. I wonder how much real effect we had in the local services. Dr David Jones, who was later made a Fellow of the Royal College of General Practitioners for his work in developing the GP hospitals in Clwyd and later still made a Professor of the University of Wales, was a valuable member as an Executive Officer of the Health Authority.

It was about 1962, when working with over 3000 patients in the surrounding 300 square miles I joined the Royal College of General Practitioners, which opened the door to many things allied to the practice. I used to join a cousin of my mother's, from Nefyn, at meetings in the Postgraduate Education Centre in Liverpool on certain Sundays. We were, to my knowledge, the only GPs from North Wales attending. I was put on the Merseyside and North Wales Faculty Board, meeting in Liverpool. Later I was elected to be Provost of the Board. This encouraged me to split from the Merseyside Faculty and form a North Wales Faculty, to lead research in general practice and education in North Wales. A drug firm financed medallions to be worn by both the Provost and Chairman. I wore each in turn. I became a member of the Welsh Council of the Royal College of General Practitioners, meeting usually in Cardiff but once in my surgery as the Chairman.. I was its Treasurer for about fifteen years and its first North Wales Chairman, lasting three years in the Post. The object of the Council was to encourage and help with the functions of the Faculties.

I immediately followed the Professor of General Practice, Cardiff Medical School,Prof Robert Harvard Davies, as Chairman of the Welsh Council while earlier my old friend, the late Dr John Owen, of Porthcawl, had been Chairman. He and I were the only

GPs who were members of the White Order of Druids of the Gorsedd of the National Eisteddfod of Wales. I recall we were sitting in a hotel in Llandrindod Wells, drinking gins at a meeting, when a female reporter from a London medical newspaper attended. She must have been the least attractive of any woman we had ever seen. John said to me - perhaps as a warning, "She gets more attractive with every gin and tonic!" The demon drink! Don't say that you haven't been warned!

I gave the Professor a cucumber from my greenhouse as a memento of his Chair. Dr Derek Llewellyn of Bridgend gave me some sand in a small medicine bottle from the sand dunes at Merthyr Mawr when he took over from me in the Chair. I had once told him that Mari and I used to picnic there! In time I was put on the Sub-Committee in General Practice of the Welsh Medical Committee, which developed and supervised postgraduate GP education and the vocational training of GPs in Wales.

As Chairman of the Welsh Council I sat on the Central Council of the College of GPs in London about four times a year and would attend an annual formal dinner, with drinks beforehand. I recall feeling so proud, standing alone against the wall of the reception room admiring well-known names of various medical organisations, when a stranger entered late and came up to me, asking me who I was. I told him and asked him who he was. He admitted to being the then Secretary of State for Health - Patrick Jenkins!

In 1975, while a single-handed GP, I was invited by a member to join the local Rotary Club. You are expected to attend at least 65 per cent of lunch-time meetings. I thought it would be impossible but tried. I almost had 100 per cent attendance on Tuesdays. In 1983 I became the President and had the Secretary of State for Wales, Mr (now Sir) Wyn Roberts to be my guest speaker at the Seventy Degrees Hotel (in his patch!). Nineteen clubs sent representatives. I started the scheme to have one evening meeting a month, as a trial. Now we always meet in the evenings once a week and help to discuss all manner of things here and abroad. Oddly enough, I have never been into a local pub for a drink other than with Rotary. It is a leftover from my Sunday School days when we were brainwashed with the evils of alcohol. All these experiences broadened my knowledge of how the Health Service was run.

Belonging to the local Rotary Club brought me in contact with many interesting characters - though possibly a third were patients of mine. It was, and is, an all male club - a very important feature to most of us. Through Rotary we develop friendships and help local and international charities. We meet on Tuesday evenings. The venues have changed over the years from each of the two biggest hotels in the town, to the Freemason's Hall, and now to a restaurant on the outskirts of the town. Each member is expected to become the President for the year - it is the 'making' of many shy men. I have had a couple wanting a 'doctor's note' to dodge their turn. This is understood. We get very interesting speakers at times, two or three weeks out of four, for 20 minutes after the meal. It is through the contact with local Rotarians that I had been asked to speak at four particular venues - the Welsh Health Authorities' Annual Dinner, the Dolgellau Rotary Charter night, the High School Annual Form 6 Dinner, and prize giving at St Bridget's Convent School.

One of the most important functions that we run is the 'Annual World Roll the Barrel Competition' - empty beer barrels are rolled around an area on the High Street on Boxing Day, after the Flint and Denbigh Hunt have left. We make quite a nice sum of money for the Denbigh Aged and Disabled Fund and our charity fund from this well-attended event.

One of the funniest things that occurred was at one of our Charter Nights. A local Church in Wales Canon was speaking when a member crept out to urinate. As he returned the Canon asked him if he could hear his voice from he toilet. He replied not - to which the Canon said, "Very strange, because we could hear you!"

A few years ago I was, as I mentioned, the guest speaker at the Annual Dinner of all the Administrators of the Health Service in Wales. About the same year I was the guest speaker at the Past Medical Students' Annual Dinner in Cardiff. I suppose I have taken the guest speaking role in a few Postgraduate Centres in Wales, in Rotary Charter nights in Colwyn Bay, Bala and Dolgellau, Leagues of Friends of Glan Clwyd Hospital Annual General Meeting and Abergele Hospital, together with many chapels, Ivy Clubs etc. One memorable reunion was in the school at Pentrevoelas; there was a minimal introduction to the Old People's Society and an hour later, at the end, a retired Minister came to me and thanked me personally, apologising that he enjoyed the talk but could not hear it as he had Glaucoma! (an eye disease).

One one occasion I had to represent the interests of the Mentally Handicapped for the Royal College Council of GPs of the UK and joined the MPs to teach them, at a party on the terrace of the Houses of Parliament. I am President of both the local Mencap Society and the Gateway Club, so have some insight into their problems and have a severely mentally handicapped son, Owen.

Possibly, this was what caused the then Secretary of State for Wales, Mr Wyn Roberts, to ask me to sit with a group of twelve or so to set up the All Wales Strategy for the Mentally Handicapped, an interesting experience although I resigned after two years as it was too time consuming. I was the only GP in the group, with people from Housing, Social Services, parents and others. Two of us addressed a meeting of interested people in Cardiff. I felt quite inadequate amongst them.

I have been President of the Camera Club, Rotary Club, Dahlia Society, and still am President of the Denbigh and Clwyd Angling Association, the local Stroke Club, Mencap, Gateway Club and the local Liberals, for the last 25 years or so. Until recently, I was President of the local Garden Produce Associates but am now Patron. My most recent post is Chairman of the Gorsedd Committee for the 2001 Eisteddfod, to be held here in Denbigh, a post my father held in 1939! As President of the Garden Produce Association, who run the Denbigh Flower Show under the indomitable Councillor Emrys Williams as Secretary, I remembered that I had once heard of a 'Lord Denbigh'. I looked him up in an 1889 Burke's Peerage book which I had inherited. The Directory Enquiries refused to give me his telephone number until I tried again the following day. I spoke to his recently widowed mother who put me in touch. He and his delightful young wife came and stayed the night with us after attending the Flower Show. We had a dinner with my family that night. The highlight of the jovial meal was Lady Denbigh showing my son Rhys and me a tattoo on the top of her left thigh, a scar she had refused to show the doctor at a Blood Transfusion Centre.

After seven years in General Practice we had our three children in turn: Rhys in 1966, Owen (the handicapped one, who is currently in sheltered employment, making garden furniture and very happy) and Elin, now a mother, farmer's wife and Matron of a local Nursing Rehabilitation Home. Rhys married Nathalie, a beautiful Lebanese Christian young lady, with a law degree. He is a scientist with a Welsh Honours BSc, a self-employed Consultant to firms such as Vodaphone, Ericsson, and Motorola, advising on the use of radio frequencies for mobile phones in India, Jordan, South Africa, Lebanon, the Czech Republic and, more recently, Brazil. Initially, he had planned to do medicine and went for interview to Cardiff. I noticed that an old colleague of mine, when he was a young doctor in Cardiff, was then Professor of Child Health - Professor Peter Gray. I took Rhys, a devout anti-Christ in those days, to meet the Professor - a devout Christian. He was interested to meet Rhys from a Welsh Medium School. Then I recalled that Rhys had gone to an English Sunday School for a few weeks once; so I mentioned it. Peter Gray asked Rhys what was discussed there, to which Rhys replied, "Third World, atomic warfare - then the subject turned to Jesus so I packed it up!' In spite of this he got in, until failing his Anatomy Exam when he switched to Physics. He had been a very enthusiastic Radio Ham since I introduced him to a keen, local amateur. In fact, while a 16 year old he spent two days and nights, alone in a tent on top of one of the mountains in the Clwydian Range with an aerial, in a competition to contact as many other stations as he could. He later became the first person from North Wales to bounce a message in Very Short Wave off the moon, in a cloudy sky, to a man in Florida. My investment of £100 in a mast in the garden was a good investment for the rest of his career all over the world. Elin did her nurse training RGN in Cardiff too. Her four year old son, Sam, is a joy to us, his grandparents and he should go far in life. He is bright and a charmer. Joshua, his baby brother, will be a pal for him.

A second cousin, Ted Thomas, has helped me in the garden for a day a week for the last 30 years. A good worker, he stole the show in a 'Cefn Gwlad' TV programme in which my family appeared for half an hour, by doing his imitation of sheep and hens etc.

My father had started a branch surgery in Bodfari and then one ten miles away, in Llansannan. He abandoned the former after some years but Llansannan is still going. Between us we missed three Tuesday evenings in about 60 years and two of those were mine! It was the snow which blocked the road. We would see, on

Dr. Mari outside the family home, Ystrad Isa.

Opening of new surgery premises, Denbigh.
Dr. Peter Elliott and Dr. Tim Peskett,
Nerys Hughes (author's second cousin, the TV star) and Dr. Gwyn Thomas.

Off to Garden Party at Buckingham Palace, 1992.
Dr. Mari, Gwyn and Elin outside HQ of R.C.G.P.

Chairman of Welsh Council R.C.G.P. 1980-1983.

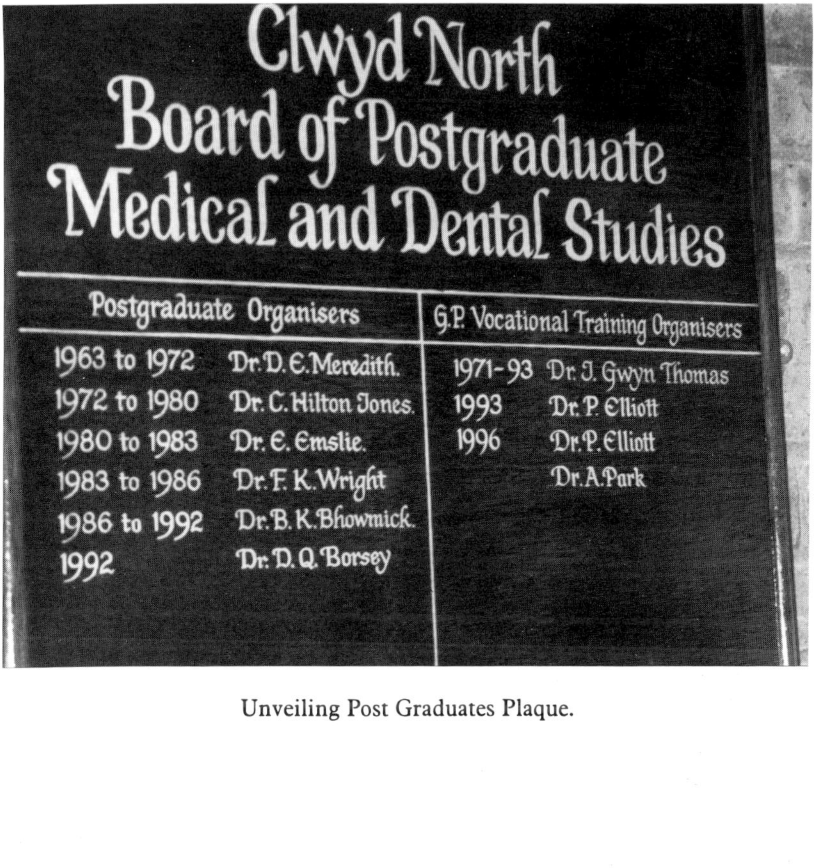

Unveiling Post Graduates Plaque.

Welsh Council Royal College of G.P.'s in Bronyffynnon.

Past Post Graduates Organisers and Gwyneth Stringfellow. c. 1992 Ysbyty Glan Clwyd.

Dr J. Gwyn Thomas. White Robe Bard 1997.
For Services to Medical Education in Wales.

Author and Professor Robert Owen.

Old student friends. Christmas 1985.
Tudor Williams (great grandson of Thomas Gee – Consultant Anaethetist);
Jane (ex Nursing Sister) Owen (Brain Surgeon); Sian (Lawyer) and
Huw (advisor to Canadian government).

Dr. Mari Thomas (author's wife).

Male cousins. Cyffylliog side.
Scientist, G.P, Barrister at Law, Dental Surgeon, Bone Specialist.

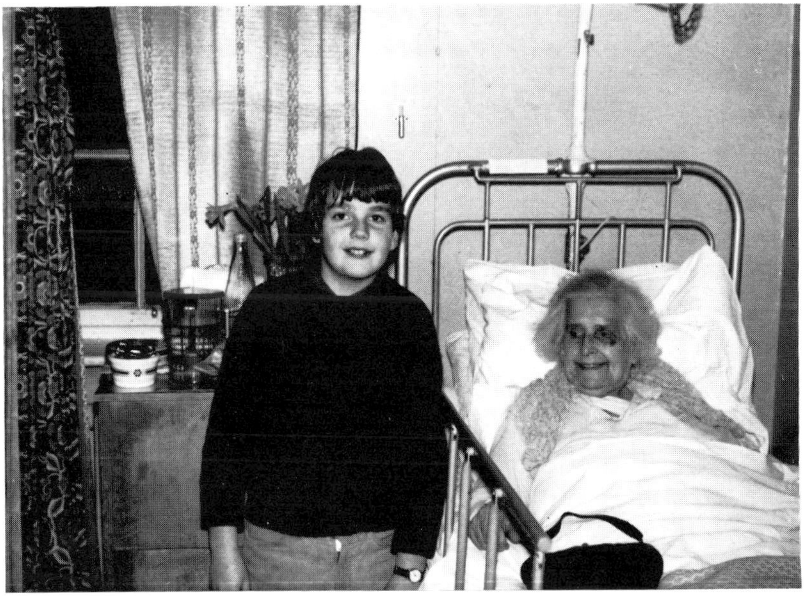

Rhys Thomas (son) with Dr. Kate Roberts at Denbigh Infirmary.

Author with wife and family. Rhys, Owen and Elin. 1987.

Picnic in North Wales.
(Owen at work that day)

an average, ten patients a session, sometimes only one or two in the summer. We had the medicines locked up in a cupboard and carried the patients' notes with us. A local mentally handicapped man, known to all as Batman, would wait for me to help carry the stuff in from my car, sit in the waiting room and help me back. He was very useful and at times would come with me on visits afterwards, sometimes at 9 or 10 o'clock at night to open the farm gates.

From the surgery I would visit patients until late at night, in my father's tradition. I would perform minor operations in their homes if they were unable to come to the surgery - held once in a front room, a Scout Hall, billiard hall, and finally in the brand new surgery built to my plan and paid for by John Evan Morris' family (Rhyd y Cilgwyn, Rhewl) as he had made a fortune in the sugar and tea importation trade in Liverpool and was from the area as a child. There was an opening ceremony on the Tuesday afternoon with local councillors and important people there. I rang the bell to admit the first patient that evening. A coloured girl of 20 years from Denbigh was the first. She had come there especially to see me. The next was a local elderly gentleman most upset, as he had been looking forward to being the first in for months! I telephoned Mr Evan Morris that evening and told him the story. I pointed out that it was just, that a girl from the Caribbean should be the first, as it was through them that he had made his money.

I mentioned minor operations. I used to call on an old farmer every three months to stick a large syringe needle into his watery filled scrotum, in front of the open fire, to aspirate the fluid out. A most satisfying job!

The butcher's wife would sometimes sit to wait her turn to come in, carrying a basket. She would take the towel off the top of the basket on coming in to me, then lay out a table cloth on the desk and put out sandwiches and tea for me. She thought I was not being looked after at home! She was a lovely, kind lady. On one occasion a letter was sent to the Minister of the Chapel and a couple of others, declaring that a certain lady took down her knickers when alone with a visiting minister and that I should put the letter writer in the Mental Hospital. Although the writer was an odd lady, I had heard elsewhere that what she wrote was true; so I really could not Section the lady.

One of my many patients there, in Llansannan, had died and as the money collected at the funeral was to be spent on the surgery, I felt I should go to the funeral. There was a huge queue to get into the chapel so that already they were going through to the schoolroom. The singing is not as good when you are tucked away but, as I filed past the Deacon's seat, one of the four ministers standing there winked at me and invited me to join them, which I did. I felt I had known the deceased better than any of the four. I enjoyed the singing. At the conclusion I phoned home from the kiosk to enquire of my wife whether anything was wanted and told her what had happened, that I had slept in the Deacon's seat and woke to find the chapel empty. She believed me!

Llansannan was my second home. I was very fond of the locals there. One of my saddest moments there was when a real young Liverpudlian came to rent the first of what was to be a row of homes for Welsh speakers. She was a young mother of two when she had to go to Broadgreen Hospital in Liverpool for a bypass operation on her heart. She did well but soon had to return for further surgery. She died on the operating table.

About twenty-five years ago a boy of eight, with a gypsy background, needed an operation on his kidneys but the family would not allow him to go to Alderhey Hospital in Liverpool on his own. I had a brainwave. Although now living in a Council house, they had the old caravan parked nearby. I found a convent near the hospital and phoned the Mother Superior asking if they had a garden site for a caravan for a couple of weeks. She agreed and all went well. The Mother Superior used to send Christmas cards to the family for years after. The illiterate parents could not reply. Strangely enough, that eight year old's eight year old son has recently been to the same hospital with kidney trouble.

A middle-aged man, a relation of mine by marriage, went to have a coronary bypass when they were first started, about 30 years ago, in Broadgreen Hospital. He had gone privately, ready for the operation the following day. Unfortunately, he died in the hospital the night before the operation. Things have improved since.

Some people do not want to hear bad news and you play a game, as it were, with them. They know you know their prognosis and don't ask; nor would I volunteer it unless some major, family thing were dependent on it. I remember a Merchant Navy Captain who, living at home with his wife, had a terminal cancer of the bowel. We acted it out and finally he died at home in the Autumn. At

Christmas time his widow came to see me with a bottle of rum. She explained that her husband had wanted me to have it, "even if he had gone!" You can treat the symptoms without volunteering the cause of them. It is often easier for the doctor to be absolutely frank, giving the prognosis coldly and then sitting back. In the same way, somehow, it is easier to deal with an elderly, confused person than one who can discuss to a degree and try to influence your handling of the case.

Then an 11 year old only child, a patient of mine, was finally diagnosed as having a brain abscess and he died on the operating table, in Walton Hospital. His father was a farm labourer and his mother a chronic schizophrenic. This was before brain scanners were available.

These are all sad but one has one's private laughs. One in particular was a lady who complained that her private parts twitched often. This was a symptom I had never seen or heard of. So I told her that just like eyes sometimes twitch when tired, her private parts are probably doing the same, so give it a rest.

Another time, on the front of the blue forms we used to confirm that patients had been immunised against Smallpox before going abroad. Apart from the name and address, it asked for an M for male or an F for female in a box labelled 'sex'. I'd show this to the potential holiday-maker and asked if they intended having sex on holiday, putting a tick or nought, depending on how they answered.

A local watch-maker's marriage lasted a week. He spent the rest of his career standing at the door of his shop with his hands in his pockets, watching the girls go by. He got older and older. Finally I admitted him to a Retirement Home. After a few weeks the matron rang me complaining that he had a habit of sitting next to a confused old lady with a tremor of Parkinsonism in her hands and he'd put her hands over his fly and spend the day red in the face. I advised the matron to ignore him as the lady didn't know what she was doing. The matron, cross with me, said that it was most embarrassing at visiting times!

Itinerant workers, often Irish, would come to Denbigh to stack corn and pick potatoes. They'd stay in a lodging house in Henllan Street for six pence a night. Iron bunk beds, one fireplace and one tap - cold and outside in the yard - was their luxury. One particular one would come to my father, who acted often as a solicitor, helping patients with wills and lending cash. One would leave his black, patent leather shoes with my father for the loan of ten shillings. At the end of the job, he'd buy them back. Unfortunately, my father died and the man never returned. I have a pair of size 10 patent leather shoes for sale.

A tramp lived with his head and shoulders under a bent bit of corrugated sheet, on a field in Llanefydd, until someone left a car for him to live in with his two cats. Once, with chest pain, he crawled to a nearby farm and I was sent for. He wore about three dirty vests and three shirts. The nurses in the Royal Alexandra Hospital must have had a job to clean him up. While he was there I was asked to chair a concert, in a nearby chapel, and asked if the congregation would contribute towards buying a garden hut for him. They refused, saying he would sell it for alcohol. By luck, a day or two later I was called to the local pub to see the injured publican and told him the saga of the tramp, named Alec. "Leave it to me," he said. Within two days, Alec was home with the hut and I had cadged a chemical toilet and bed for him. He was as pleased as Punch when I visited him. I remember seeing a rabbit's snare on a nail on the wall.

A few months later, as no one had seen him, I called there on a very dark night and with the help of a torch saw the door was open. The two cats leaped out, giving me a fright, and there was Alec dead across his bed. I could swear that he had a smile on his face. The villagers paid for a nice gravestone for him and a poem pointing out that he had been a sniper in the First World War. I have a cutting from the local paper describing how he had been convicted of stealing a hen from a farm, in the 1940s.

I remember being very worried about a schoolboy, the son of a good, hardworking family, who had become an alcoholic at the age of 15 years. I tried all ways to change his ways. He left school, found a job in a local shop for a few years, then went off to London. I felt that was the end of him. About 12 years later, I was standing waiting to be served my fish and chips in a local shop when a voice behind me demanded that he pay for my order! It was the same person - now the manager of a big store in London!

On another occasion, a 15 year old schoolboy came to see me to ask for a doctor's note to excuse him the cane he was to suffer that afternoon. He wanted the note to declare that he had a stomach ulcer - which he had. I asked if he minded if I spoke to the Head, a friend of mine. I told the Head what the boy - sitting at my side - wanted him to know regarding the ulcer and told him it was wrong to cane the boy. "Worst boy in the school!" was the reply. I gave him my opinion that he was worst as he was different and these are the 'leaders of tomorrow'. We couldn't agree. He was caned. I watched the boy's progress. He became a Senior Nurse in the Mental Hospital.

A story with a sad ending was that of a youngish farmer who lived alone with his wife and was struck with severe Parkinsonism. He could only move his right thumb and lay in bed all day, depending on his wife popping in to see him periodically. In my workshop I connected a front door bell push to a battery and bell and set them by his bedroom window. He was able to press the bell from bed when he wanted her. Then the drug L-dopa became available. Within six months he was walking into chapel and able to speak to his mother. I noticed one day that his wife looked overtired and asked her to come to see me. I could feel the cancer mass in her abdomen, which killed her very soon. His last days were spent in a Council Home - and the drug showed unfortunate side effects.

Apart from the accidents that I mentioned earlier, I recall three consultations in particular. I had managed to walk up Snowdon with the children about 20 years ago, along the Miners' Track. Having reached the top, a patient of mine, a 40 year old, found me puffing away and said he would like to see me quite seriously on the Monday, as he was short of breath. Another, an 18 year old and quite a character in the town, had pains in his belly as he lay on top of a haystack and refused to come down. He worked on the farm. The ambulance had also been called. I climbed up a ladder to the patient to examine him there and decided - later it was confirmed - that he had appendicitis. This was removed successfully, after he had been coaxed down. The strangest was at my father's funeral when a local tenor, an elderly man, conducted the singing at his graveside, by my side. As the coffin was being lowered he turned to me and asked if I had a prescription with me, as he had a cough. Would you believe it?

Soon after my father's funeral I planted a Peace rose on the grave, as he was fond of roses. There had been a lot of well-justified admiration of him at his funeral. However, very soon I got a letter from the Parish Council asking me to move the rose as it made cutting the grass difficult. My first reaction was to refuse; then I thought better of it. I phoned my vet. friend to join me on a secret mission in the pitch dark at the cemetery. I asked him to carry the pick-axe and a spade. He was astounded as I started digging over my father, and lights came on in nearby cottages as he held the torch. To his relief, he heard my tale of woe and we went home to transplant the rose in my garden.

He, Gwynn Llywelyn, mainly wrote the words to a song in Welsh "Y Dan Feddyg Cymraeg". We sang it, as a duet at the retirement of Professor Robert Owen, in Conwy, in a restaurant. Gwyneth, his talented teacher wife, played the piano and we have given a number of recitals since.

One Monday night as I was leaving the surgery, a police car shot past me followed by an ambulance. I followed them, asking bystanders which turning they took ending up 6 miles away in a farm yard. The farmer had fallen into a huge tank of corn as the auger lifted the grain. His right arm was at the far end of the tank - loose! I was able to inject morphine to his other arm while the Fire Service lifted him out and the arm was put in a black plastic bin bag, to be transported to the hospital. He was not a patient of mine but, by coincidence I next saw him at the Mental Hospital where he was suffering from depression. I recognised him by his missing arm. He thanked me.

CHAPTER 7

General Practice

Tales

I had at one time chaired the Parent Teacher Association at the 1500 strong Welsh medium Secondary School, which was short of books. Two of my children were pupils. I suggested that parents be invited to contribute, if they could, £1 a term towards a library. The teachers objected, saying it was the place of the Local Education Authority to fund them. I thought them very short-sighted. It has become the norm now. At this time my daughter needed 5 'O' levels to go nursing. The teachers told me she wouldn't get two. I asked my friend the Head to keep her down a year as her birthday was 31 August - she couldn't be younger. Against my instincts, I transferred her to a private girls' school - the only time I have never slept all night. However, she got 9 'O' levels and a husband, the brother of her best friend, in the new school. It was at that private school during the prize giving that I stood up and suggested that a place on the governing body should be allocated to a representative of fee-paying parents. The incestuous Governors refused - and the status quo exists now.

It was before we knew that our slow-learner son was a Slow Learner that I was made President of the local Mencap Group, (with Mari later the Chairman) and also the Gateway Club. We had started running coffee evenings, on the last Friday in June, 31 years ago with the great help of the local society, in particular Mrs Mair Silyn Jones. Although, at first, the tickets to enter the house and garden, with coffee and biscuits supplied, were two shillings, while now it is 50p, regularly we made the equivalent of £1,000 for the cause. The last time it was £1,420. There are stalls for cakes, old clothes, vegetables and games - supported by our local Rotary Club and chapels.

I was asked once to take part in a Welsh TV programme in Bangor on 'Obesity' before an audience, to which I agreed. The audience was asked by the compere what they thought the overweight man's work was: I trust that no one knew my real job when they called out "Butcher!"

I was reminded recently of when, as a young doctor, I was sorry for a couple living in a Council house, as they were getting married and could not afford a wedding breakfast. Their two children lived in the same house. I went to the owner of a local biscuit factory, told their story and cadged a big tin of chocolate biscuits to give the party. Nice to be able to do it.

A middle-aged, very clean widow lived in a two-up-and-two-down terraced cottage. She had about six children, mainly by different fathers. She would offer men a boiled egg at her house after a chat in a local pub. She would serve the boiled egg in her bed upstairs and a daughter the same on the couch downstairs. This prevailed for years until she had a severe stroke and it was doubtful that she would survive the night in her bed. She was unconscious. Her children were gathered downstairs. A new young minister had arrived in the town and I asked him to come with me to the house. I asked the children if they would like a service by the new man. He was very nice to them all and we all went upstairs for a service around the bed. Looking up I saw a black and white etching of Jesus on the cross above the bed. It crossed my mind as to how many randy men had gone up those stairs and failed with the thought of the Lord watching. I was pleased to hear the minister tell me years later that it was the best job he had ever done as, in the minds of the children, he had cleansed her before she died early next morning.

A few years ago I was in the barbers having a haircut when my receptionist rushed in to say there was an emergency in a Council house in an outlying village. I rushed there to find the father of eight children - a newcomer - standing in his pyjamas in the bedroom with a plastic bag of ice cubes held over his scrotum. He was an extremely religious man, and toured Wales in his white double decker bus preaching, with, 'God will save you?' written on the body of the bus. It appeared that he had been unfaithful to his wife in the past and, after a discussion with his wife, decided to cut off his penis as instructed in the Bible. He put a piece of elastic band around the base, chopped the rest off with the specially sharpened carving knife and threw the loose end into the fire (though the Alsatian dog looked happy!) He refused an ambulance to take him to the District General Hospital; so I had to put an empty plastic sack on the front seat of my brand new car to protect it from blood and took him to the Infirmary. The nurses were quite upset when I threw back the blanket I had covered him with. He wanted to urinate; so I passed a catheter, with success. He refused an injection of morphine but accepted an anti-tetanus injection. I had put the morphine in with the A-T serum and soon he was drowsy enough to transfer to the District General Hospital, where he was tidied up. He discharged himself that night. His next problem was erotic ideas with erections in the stump. He requested that his testes be removed. No surgeon would do it without the encouragement of a psychiatrist. Two refused, saying he was not 'mental'. He would go for a run up in the hills when aroused!

Two months later his wife asked me to call. He was in his darkened bedroom having cut open his scrotum with a penknife and taken a big dose of Valium. He went by ambulance post-haste to the big hospital. They stitched him, he discharged himself and I never saw him again. He packed his bus and drove off with his children. It was discussed on TV and in the newspapers.

It was about this time that I drove the President of the Royal College of General Practitioners from Cardiff to my house for the night, before his going on to Edinburgh. I was 'on call' at 1 p.m. and it was then 12.55 p.m. as I sped at 70 mph on the 60 mph road, near home, when stopped by my ex-partner's 'speed cop' son. I appeared in Court with a solicitor who pleaded my case. As we left the Court at 10 a.m., fined £80, I assured the solicitor that it was the best job he'd done that day - jokingly. I had his bill for £60 the following day, on which he'd written, 'My second-best job today!'

I am called periodically to the Mental Health Unit to certify patients, as I am recognised by the Mental Health Act to do this. You need a hospital psychiatrist and a person not involved with the hospital to do this, after investigating the poor person. A social worker is also involved. It is quite interesting work, not lucrative, but you meet old friends on the staff. The patient can appeal legally against your opinion if you have 'Sectioned' him, ('certify' is the old term). My cousin Haf's solicitor son is the person called in on behalf of the patient. Once one warm sunny afternoon I was listening to a young man giving me his symptoms - we were sitting at the hospital window - and I fell asleep. The patient woke me asking if I was all right!

I was once called by a social worker to Deeside, 24 miles away, as they couldn't find a doctor qualified to section an elderly lady locking herself indoors there. Most patients are manic-depressive, schizophrenic, or demented people but, more and more, one sees youngsters with brains affected by drugs. I recall being called to a ground floor flat by an elderly lady as 'water' was dripping through from the locked flat above her, which was occupied by a patient of mine. I broke down the door of this alcoholic to find him drunk, stuck in his chair, glued by his faeces with a bottle of whisky overturned nearby.

A local lady window cleaner, who was usually drunk, told me that whenever she cleaned the windows of one local man he was always standing in the bedroom window exposing himself.

A sideline which I had been doing for years, after the post of Factory Doctor was discontinued, meant visiting people, most previously unknown to me, who had applied for a Disabled Living Allowance. To qualify, they have to fail to be able to do certain things when you examine them. It gave me an insight into conditions in Rhyl, very different from my Practice. I thank God I practised in the rural area that I did. I knocked on the door of one terraced house in the West End of Rhyl, to be confronted by the 60 year old drunk - the candidate. He invited me up, but not to his room as he had defecated (or a word to that description) in his bed and we'd go to the flat on his landing, next door to his, occupied by an alcoholic lady. While taking the history I asked him if he had ever taken drugs, at which he grabbed my lapels and spat in my face, "for suggesting that!" I very nearly gave the job up at that, as I had my pension and didn't need the £40 or so that it paid for at least two hours' work – less tax.

Apart from that, for the Allowance, I examined some very nice people along the coast mostly elderly who had gone there on holiday, in earlier years, from the Midlands, Manchester or Liverpool and retired to one of the many bungalows there. A few would promise to send me a postcard from their holidays and would do so, only to find that they had been turned down from that financial reward. One young lady I visited lived in a derelict farm. I shouted on my arrival at the front door. Her child was in school. A reply came from up the dark stairs - mid-day! I found the applicant lying on a mattress on the floor under a sheet, underclothes on the floor, no furniture except the mattress. I put my square case on the mattress and lay on my left side, at right angles to the lady, leaning on my left elbow and took the history. It was on my way home I realised what a position I would have been in if she complained to a Court that I had done anything incorrect. "Yes, my Lord! He was lying on my mattress with me!" It would have cost me more than the £40 I earned.

I remember well how, as a young doctor, a certain woman came to see me as she thought she was pregnant. I told her that I wanted to examine her and went out of my room to collect some papers. When I returned she was standing naked, her limbs outstretched, in the middle of my consulting room. I advised her. Blow me, she did the same thing a month later at the second consultation!

For about ten years my wife, Mari, consulted in the room next to mine. A man whom I had warned her about, as he had allegedly been interfering with little girls of neighbours, went in to her. He had complained that his penis bent in double when erected, (a recognised medical condition). Before examining him she told him that a medical student, who was with me, would be interested to see this phenomenon. He was, she believed, expecting a young female - not the huge rugger player from Cardiff who came in with me. He told me that a box had fallen on it. He had no reply when I asked him what his penis was doing out when reaching for the box. I saw him 25 years later - entering the surgery. "Who does he go to now?" I wonder.

We accepted medical students from Liverpool, Manchester or Cardiff University for one to four weeks. Occasionally they would be sons or daughters of friends of ours. You would give them tasks to do - for example injecting, or suturing lacerations. Even feeling for the prostate gland may be the only chance they have during their undergraduate career to do this. I had had my father to teach me.

One of the early students, unknown to me, was making a record of all the cases he saw in a month and he wrote a prize winning article in the *Journal of the Royal College of General Practitioners.* He went off to Canada later when qualified.

Friends' sons from Calgary, Canada, came to me for a fortnight;

another came from Sydney, Australia. Both are neurosurgeons now, by coincidence. One learnt and had a lot of pleasure from having students. They would stay with us, or in the Nurses' Home of the Infirmary, or the Mental Hospital Nurses' Home.

I felt someone should update the history booklet of the Infirmary with the blessing of the Chairman of the Health Authority, that great local public benefactor Mr Michael Griffith, CBE, DL, of Trefnant, who agreed that they would pay for it. I've updated it twice, with the help of the Hospital Secretary, to be sold for the profit of the League of Friends. Another booklet I wrote was of my memories of my schooldays in Denbigh during the 1939/45 War. The sale, at £1 per copy, gave the Eisteddfod fund a nice fillip of £400. The idea was initiated by Mr Gwyn Dodd, the Head of the local High School, after a chat in the Rotary Club.

High Court Judge, William Mars Jones, had come to my parents for supper one night when he was in the Navy. He brought his beautiful ballet dancer girlfriend with him. At one stage, she excused herself and went upstairs to the toilet, when she slipped and cut her head quite badly. My father took her to the surgery in the back of the house and stitched it with a huge cutting needle and horsehair kept in methylated spirits. The friendship with the girl soon stopped. Was it the scar, I wonder!

A collection of my old, inherited medical instruments stimulated me to try to establish a Welsh Medical Museum and at the same time Professor Sir Bernard Knight, the famous Forensic Pathologist I have previously mentioned, was thinking along the same lines. A Trust of ten people, four from Northern and six from Southern Wales, have been meeting and looking at potential sites in both parts of Wales. After a most interesting visit to the Medical Museum in Leeds we modified our ambitions but are still meeting to pursue it.

It was not very often that people wasted my time, but I can recall a middle aged lady from a nearby estate transferring to me from a local practice as she was unhappy with the attention she had! She had absolutely nothing wrong with her and I was unable to locate any reason – occult or not, for her visits – pre-appointments time. She came about twice a week for about 18 months. She came in once and complained that she was 'feeling buggard'! I was particularly busy at the time and agreed with her saying 'You are buggard!' She was accepted back by her previous practice.

I was suspicious once at my Llansannan surgery that a middle aged lady was attending for flippant reasons and at the same time a local farmer – unlike his pattern, was doing the same at the same surgeries. Time soon disclosed the reason – using my surgery as an excuse to get to the village to liaise.

CHAPTER 8

General Practice

The Latter Years and Today

In the 1960s, the late Dr David Meredith, in charge of postgraduate medical education, in Rhyl asked me to share the 'stage' with a Professor of Medicine from Guy's. He was the world authority on Diabetes. I was to speak on 'Diabetes in General Practice'. That encouraged me. He then asked me to arrange GP postgraduate evenings. I would telephone about four General Practitioners and tell them they had been selected to talk about one of their patients. Little did they know that the selection was done by me and not some august academic body! The first to speak was a well-known authoritarian GP from Ffynnongroew, who presented a case that had been misdiagnosed by Dr Meredith himself - it was the GP's wife. That didn't go down too well, as can be imagined.The system worked well for about four evenings a year, for four or five years. It became mandatory for GPs to attend a certain number of the postgraduate sessions if they wished to qualify for their pensions.

It was because of this experience, I suppose, that I set up the first Vocational Training Scheme for aspiring Family Doctors in Wales, after serving on the setting up of the Welsh Pilot Scheme in Bridgend under the umbrella of the Postgraduate Department of the Welsh National School of Medicine, as it was then known. Mr Aldis, a Consultant Surgeon and an old teacher of mine, was Head of the latter and Dr Derek Llewellyn became first Regional Advisor in General Practice for Wales. We worked closely for 23 happy years, I as the North Clwyd Course Organiser.

This meant finding appropriate practices in North Wales to train young doctors in the art of general practice and also useful hospital posts. They would spend a year in general practice, then six months in each of selected hospital departments for two years. At first, Consultants were suspicious of the scheme but soon accepted it as routine, as they would receive a continuous, safe source of Senior House Physicians or Surgeons, two annually at first, then four, selected sometimes from 40 to 50 applicants to the scheme. Mr David Aiken, Consultant Obstetrician and Gynaecologist, would sit with me to select ten or twelve to come for an interview, which I later chaired. Six hospital doctors and six trainer GPs would sit together to interview the candidates, a testing time for the anxious people. During the 23 years that I ran the scheme, others were started in Wrexham and Bangor. Possibly well over 100 GP doctors were trained on my scheme and most have settled down nearby. Only two did not end up in general practice; one went to London to do Alternative Medicine while the other has become a valuable, local Consultant Paediatrician. We would meet together on Thursday afternoons at Ysbyty Glan Clwyd and pursue a programme I had arranged with the most valuable help of the Postgraduate Department Administrator, Mrs Gwyneth Stringfellow. Occasionally, we would visit somewhere strange but valuable, for example a coal mine pit face, or Ambulance Headquarters control room. As a medical student I had seen two pit faces in South Wales - but the Point of Ayr still frightened me as sparks flew from the drills. It was a delight to see over a hundred ex-Trainees of mine at the dinner which drug companies paid for, at my retirement as Course Organiser at the Seventy Degrees Hotel in Colwyn Bay.

During this time, and unknown to me, I was recommended by Merseyside doctors to be elected a Fellow of the Royal College of General Practitioners - the first in North Wales to have this honour. It meant going to London where we stayed with Nerys Hughes, of Liver Birds fame, my second cousin. She came to the ceremony at a large Hall in BMA House. Little did she think then that she would become a Fellow of the University of Bangor in the year 2000.

In 1998 I had the idea of collecting together the surviving Thomases, descending from my Great Grandfather, Griffith Thomas, Head Gamekeeper at Pallé Hall near Llanderfel. He was the son of the landlord of the Cross Keys Pub, there. There were three sons, Huw, Thomas and Robert. To help organisation, I gave each descendant of the three one of three coloured sticky labels. A hundred and twenty people turned up at a local hostelry, for a lunch, and a representative of each colour gave a short talk on Huw, Thomas and Robert. I felt it was great - meeting new relations. A large poster of the family tree helped.

Mari had only four cousins, two alive in London and two deceased in South Wales. Alan, now deceased, was in Planning, in Porthcawl. I have four on my mother's side - a Geography teacher, a housewife, an engineer and an orthopaedic surgeon. The latter's mother married my father's brother, also an orthopaedic surgeon. Of the paternal cousins, Medwyn, who after banking ran the village stores with his brother Huw, has died. It was with Medwyn that we had great fun in the village. His sister Beryl also worked in a bank locally. Huw was a stores manager for the County Council. I have mentioned Gwyn and Emyr Lloyd. There is Neville, a senior Queen's Counsel in London and poor old Iolo, who died in an epileptic fit, the only child of his parents. Of the next generation , there are only two doctors - Haf's son, Sion and one of my sister Gwenllian's sons, William, is following his father's profession. However, Beryl's son-in-law is a G.P. and her son is a dentist. They surely could never enjoy medicine as much as I have. Other cousins were from Roewen, in Banking, Engineering and 3 of them, housewives.

When Elin was 16 years old she wanted three items to celebrate the occasion. First was a powerful hair-dryer; second was a dinner for her and her schoolgirl friend in a specific hotel and thirdly (and the cheapest) was to see a Post Mortem. Of course, I fixed up the three and Rhys wanted to join her in the last two! The Pathologist friend phoned me the following day to say that they both had their noses stuck over the body, which was particularly smelly that day! They both enjoyed it.

At one time a fellow member of the local Angling Club had had a stroke and I felt so sorry for the self-employed plumber to be isolated at home all the time. I called the Director of Social Services to a meeting at my surgery and to gain permission to use the local Day Centre for the Elderly as a centre for a Stroke Club once a month. As the Rotary President, I selected two members of the local Club, to be Chairman and Treasurer and, with strong publicity, it was set up 15 years ago and is still going strong as the Denbigh Stroke Club - with the same officers.

One of the pleasures of retirement is that I can take my time walking over High Street now, having chats with all and sundry. I can also kiss the girls, which I had dreaded doing lest I was 'struck off'. I have my fingers in so many things now - and don't have to wear rubber gloves to do so!

Late in the year 2000 we were invited to a wonderful stage-managed night in Portmeirion, for our neighbour's 60th birthday (Gaynor Rowlandson, neé Morgan Rees). Bedrooms for sixty guests had been booked with three meals, a fly past with a banner, fireworks, a male voice choir and Carol Parry Jones and her retinue to entertain us.

At one meeting of the Liberal Executive twenty years ago, we needed a Prospective Candidate. I had heard, and admired at the Clwyd Local Medical Committee meeting, the late Dr David Williams, Holywell, a partner in my Grandfather's and Uncle's old practice, and suggested him. I was asked to enquire of him. I rang him that night asking if he was a Liberal. "I'll let you know in the morning," was his reply. He agreed and, as mentioned earlier, stood on three elections, unsuccessfully.

In my absence I was elected Chairman of the Denbigh 2001 Eisteddfod Gorsedd Committee, where I appointed 95 per cent of my Committee in a most undemocratic but friendly way. We became responsible for arranging with the Headmaster, an appointed Committee Member, how many school rooms were needed for changing, which schools were to be invited to do the dancing and play the musical instruments, the parade through the town, officials of the Eisteddfod, Bards and Druids, schools, local authority officials and representatives of local organisations, to Proclaim the Eisteddfod of a year later. We had to see that selected people had refreshments and that the gowns were distributed and in good order. The Gorsedd Stones, donated by Tarmac of Denbigh Quarry, were the responsibility of the Technical Committee. I am on that Committee, the Finance Committee and the General Committee as Chairman of the Gorsedd. I find it all fascinating.

At the Proclamation, at the beginning of July 2000, the thousand invited guests walked down Vale Street. Everyone had collected around the stones when, because of the bad weather, the Archdruid transferred the ceremony to the Sports Hall of Denbigh High School, across the field. Let not history repeat itself!

A year before I had been elected, again in my absence, to be

Chairman of the Denbigh Welsh Society. I had only been a member for two years, as I had wanted to hear a couple of speakers. Had I been present I would probably have refused as I didn't feel justified to fill such a position. In fact, it was not too daunting. I knew all the members of old.

I had, about 28 years before, called a strike by parents of the Welsh Medium Primary School and no one attended the school on the first day of term. The County Council had insisted that children, with or without their parents, crossed the main Rhyl Road rather than allow them to disembark into the perfectly safe school yard. The protest led to a confrontation, a public meeting in Ruthin Courtroom with the Chairman of the Education Committee (poor fellow had a bad chest) in the Chair, the Director of Education one side and the senior legal man, a patient of mine, the other. Governor Dr Kate Roberts, Headmistress Kate Davies, parent Gwynn Llywelyn and myself as speaker, presented our case. We lost, but protective railings were set up on the pavements to funnel the children in.

Care of the elderly is as satisfying as that of the handicapped. I recall walking through a ward at the Denbighshire Infirmary and as I passed the bed of a man of 75, he fell back and looked for all purposes as if dead. We were able to get an Electrocardiogram on to him and found a pulse of 48 a minute - a heart block. I thumped his chest, to the amazement of the other men on the ward, who hadn't realised what was going on and, when his heart got back to normal, he 'woke up' wondering what had happened. He had been admitted from Bodfari as he had 'fainted' in one of his fields. He went in and out of these attacks, and I kept thumping him, until we got him into the District General Hospital when someone else took over. He was one of the first in North Wales to have a pace-maker fitted and lived many years afterwards.

One elderly farming bachelor lived with his bachelor brother and had had treatment for cancer of the prostrate many years previouslyand, as he was rather incontinent of urine after this, had been fitted by the hospital with a penile clamp. I had forgotten this when he came to see me about five years later, when he asked for a replacement of this, "clothes-line peg, chromium and sponge gadget." I had to tell him that they were not available on a prescription but he would have to spend about £5 on a new one, from the chemist. He was shocked and asked if it was possible to obtain a second-hand one! This was, when you think of it, a reasonable request as it had saved the country a lot of money on further operations. I had the question brought up in the BMA in London, without success.

I had two cases of AIDS in my practice, when only 50 or so had been found in Wales! Both were very sad cases. One was an only child in his mid-twenties, a haemophiliac who had received infected blood a short time before. The other was a bachelor teacher, whom I had admitted to hospital. He had been wrongly diagnosed as suffering from Multiple Sclerosis and given quite the wrong drug, ACTH. Fairly early one morning we heard a knocking, at the back door, to find the Consultant Physician there explaining how it had all happened. It was a Visiting Consultant from Liverpool who had asked the pertinent question, whether the 35 year old was a homosexual, and the diagnosis and future was clear. At his funeral I was told a number of men knelt and kissed the coffin.

Really one saw very little true sexually transmitted disease in the 38 years. I recall how one lady I knew had had Syphilis and on meeting Mari for the first time, found fit to kiss her at the front door of the surgery. The other one was a local man, an ex-Service man.

It was at the front door that an odd wife of a local GP stood, in my father's time, at the bottom of the steps to the front door of the surgery and would stop patients coming in and advise them to try her husband down the other road! I don't know how effective she was.

It was in my early years that I was asked by my ex-French teacher, who had married a prominent Llansannan man, to take part in a Temperance Meeting in a local chapel to speak on the sins of alcohol. My student days tales had not caught up with her! I was flattered to be asked but don't know how influential I was while speaking to the converted. It was in the same chapel some years later that I was guest Chairman of a concert held to raise funds for the National Eisteddfod held in Ruthin, called the Dyffryn Clwyd Eisteddfod. Ties were being sold with DC printed all over them. As I was speaking I noticed a local Councillor sitting in the front of the gallery. He had organised the local fund raising and had a nickname, for some unknown reason, of Davy Crocket. It suddenly struck me to use this and I said that the organisers of the

Eisteddfod having recognised all the good work he had done had put his initials on the tie! I am not sure if he and I have been very good friends since.

My mother had told me that Mr Tom Lloyd MA, of Cyffylliog, and my father went to school together in the village of Cyffylliog and that my father was pleased that Mr Lloyd had gone to India to teach, as he was not fond of him for some reason. Oddly enough, they died within a day of each other and were buried next to each other in 1967. It is my habit to take flowers to my parents' grave at Christmas time. One year I was late and it was an evening in March that I decided, at about midnight, to take some hyacinths that I had grown in a pot. It was pitch dark. I found the grave and removed some old flowers which I had assumed my brother and sister had put there and took them to the bin, before placing my attractive flowers on the spot. I stood back to admire them in the torch light and was horrified to see that I had put them on Mr Tom Lloyd's grave - horrified as I had disposed of the old flowers put on by Mr John Grey Lloyd, his local solicitor son. I retrieved them with haste!

I tell the tale of a young lady who needed to be examined one winter's evening. I needed her clothes off for some reason. I apologised that my curtains, which act as a screen, had gone to be cleaned but that she may like to take her things off in the dark. She agreed. A voice from the dark asked where she may put her clothes - I replied that it was all right if she put them on top of mine on the chair in the corner! I hope no one believes it!

A retired local tradesman of distinguished appearance, a bachelor and known to everyone as he would attend anyone's funeral to get a free meal, was tall, thin and wore a tidy dark suit - as that was his trade - would come early to our surgery (though not a patient) and sit there throughout the morning, afternoon or evening surgery cadging cigarettes from other people in the waiting room. After the last patient went in to see the doctor he would leave. On one occasion, I grabbed him and 'operated' on his finger nails, which were like claws, and I had to use a small saw on some. It was said that he had bags of cash tucked away under his bed. I'm sure I would have been up for assault if he had complained.

A lady, not very bright, went to Dr Mari and showed her a wart on her thigh. Mari asked me to remove it in my Minor Ops session that afternoon, to which I agreed. The patient saw one of our staff on the High Street and shouted, "I'm having it off with Dr Gwyn today!" I hope no one hearing her believed it!

Someone was urinating in our empty milk bottles, left at the back door of the surgery, on Saturday nights. I suspected a drunk from a club opposite. This went on for four or five weeks, until I put a notice in the local paper, 'Will the person who is urinating in our milk bottles, presumably a man, report to his doctor as there is sugar in his urine!' It never recurred - and no patient of ours turned up with a specimen.

I had a pleasant old man of eighty who visited my branch surgery every two weeks for a few months. After some time, his wife came to apologise as there was never anything wrong with him. I reassured her that I was pleased to see him as he was a poet. She said someone had told him that, if the doctor had not seen him two weeks before he died, he would have to have a post mortem and he wanted to avoid this!

One old man lived alone in a row of Alms Houses nearby and I was called to see him as he had a cold. He had a loaded 4.10 shotgun near his back door. I asked him what that was for. He replied that his neighbour at the other end of the row came over every Spring and urinated on his row of daffodils and killed them. He was going to teach him a lesson. There was a spent cartridge stuck in the gun, so it was safe.

I had felt that the training of a doctor was incomplete in many ways. One was the relationship with undertakers and handling bereavement and the physically and mentally handicapped people. Therefore in 1979 I invited a local undertaker – Mr Ivor Howatson to do a presentation at our Thursday afternoon seminar. He brought along someone's ashes and a selection of shrouds. It went down well.

I was called from bed about 25 years ago to declare that a man had died in a narrow terraced house at the back of Mr Howatson's Chapel of Rest. As the widow needed to go back to bed, it meant moving the body out. He was wrapped in a sheet and the two of us carried him down the steep stairs, across the dark road and over the low wall to the Chapel of Rest. All part of the service!

About the same year an elderly farmer had died and lay on the kitchen floor of his son's farmhouse. The children were on the school bus on the way home. The son told me the name of his chosen Undertaker – but unfortunately he did not possess a Chapel of Rest. His opposition Undertaker, Mr Howatson, had one opposite to our G.P. Infirmary and after my coaxing agreed to let the farmer lie there. Ambulances were not allowed to carry bodies in these circumstances, but again with some coaxing of the Controller who again had been talking to the G.P. trainees in the past, he agreed to shift the body before the children arrived to the Chapel of Rest. It all went well, I was reminded of the drama by the son this month.

I had the medical student fianceé of my Orthopaedic cousin with me for a month during her training. She was staying with us. One evening, Mr Howatson rang me to say that a body for cremation lay in his Chapel of Rest and it needed a second opinion before arrangements could be made and the family doctor had nominated me for this job. Without explaining to Judy I told her to follow me to the car urgently and drove off in the night to the Chapel. Mr Howatson was at the door and pointed in the direction of the body. I told Judy, with an attitude of haste to quickly give the 'Kiss of Life'. She had not been warned as to where we were. She bent down at the head of the body to start when she realised the situation. She stood up aghast and said 'You bugger!'

CHAPTER 9

Relaxing

It has all been a very busy time. even though I worked, at first with the partner I had inherited from my father. Mari worked in Public Health and Psychiatry. My father, after about two years making a threesome practice, became gradually confused. He would come into my consulting room in his pyjamas and was found in town similarly dressed. His blood pressure had dropped during a bleed from a stomach ulcer destroying some of his brain cells. I remember calling on him in the Royal Alexandra Hospital when Mr Ivor Lewis had operated on him the day before and he had a tube up his nose to his stomach, to feed him for a few days. He asked me to get him a miniature whisky. I was horrified! One reason was that I did not believe he took alcohol and secondly was the danger of swallowing such a liquid at that stage. He was such a dominant character that I bought some from a local pub and stood behind him as he swallowed it. I was busy sucking it back with a syringe up the pipe: he caught me and played hell! A waste of money! He became an inpatient in our Denbighshire Infirmary for two years before he died. My mother died three or four years later, near the ward in which I was born.

I hope I have instilled into my lovely children a sense of humour. For instance, Elin, while rocking a baby to sleep in the Children's Ward of the Heath Hospital, Cardiff, was interrupted by a senior doctor telling her the lullaby was not very appropriate. She replied it was the one her Dad used to sing to her as a baby - "It's only me from over the sea says Bolocky Bill the Sailor!" Then I had warned her that she was not to have her new car, a 2CV, until she could afford to pay for its running costs. She was living in a Nurses' Home at Llandough Hospital, out in the country outside

Cardiff, and was shuttled in daily by bus. After a couple of months there she telephoned, very pleased with herself, as she had found a job as a barmaid at night in a pub in the village nearby. I congratulated her and advised her to keep at it, though working late there and getting up at six in the morning. A month later she rang again to tell me that she had had a pay rise as she had been promoted to the topless bar. She had the car the following day! A cunning myth!

Rhys, not keen on soccer in primary school, would dodge the ball. His white shorts were cleaner coming home than before! He would spend hours up a tree-house with a neighbour's daughter, or playing tennis against the gable end of the house. I'd had to smack him once for playing with electric plugs, with his small hands clutching them.

Rhys now working as a self-employed Consultant as an RF Design Engineer in Telecommunications who was recently in the Czech Republic but is now in Brazil, is in frequent contact by e-mail. Mari and I visited the Lebanon for a few days before returning for his wedding to the Catholic Maronite Nathalie. It was a most remarkable few days, people so excited and generous and the city of Beirut so battered. Her parents had struggled hard to put her and her sister through private education and through the Law School. Mari and I were the only two there on Rhys's side. All the expenses of the wedding and entertaining the 100 or so guests were his! Strange to us, there was no singing in the protestant Maronite church but plenty of dance music at the wedding reception.

Elin had her wedding, to farmer Richard Kellett, at Llanrhaeadr Church within our Parish. (She liked the Church environment, although christened at Capel Mawr, as all three were). The Capel Mawr Minister, Rev. W. H. Pritchard, took part. The Vicar left halfway through to get his Order of Service Book! Then after a ride in Mr Gilmore's pony and trap, we had the reception for 200 in a marquee at home, a happy day too.

Owen is as happy as a lark living with another handicapped boy, with carers, and going to work daily making garden furniture. We visit him mid-week and he is home on Sundays and holidays.

I felt that a fishing holiday was always welcome. My father had never taken a holiday in his 38 years of work and didn't expect me to need one. The partner asked me to enquire of my father if we now could have one, as there were three doctors in the practice. It was with some anxiety that I asked - and we were allowed two weeks a year. Now it is at least six. One of the most memorable fishing holidays was with Bob Owen and Meg, his wife, to County Kerry in Ireland, staying at the Butler Arms in Waterville. Bob and I would fish in a boat with a ghillie all day. Then the three of us would drink Paddy's Whiskey at the bar, have a bath, before joining our wives for a meal and billiards. It was bliss.

About four years ago my sporting cousin, Gwyn Lloyd, of Builth Wells, invited me to join him and six other men for a weekend on the Plinlimon Mountains. The other six were a mixed bag of fishermen from that part of Wales. We met sitting outside a pub in Rhayader while the more expert went to shop for sausages, eight huge steaks, vegetables and bread. One was designated to be the cook! We then drove in Landrovers and a pickup alongside the Claerwen Reservoir and then 10 miles north over the trackless moorland to the highest and loneliest dwelling south of Scotland, to Hafod y Llyn. There were two single storey wooden huts and a toilet, which was like a wooden telephone kiosk with a hole under a plank and a door kept shut by a stone. One hut had the dormitory for six and the kitchen - a gas stove, a table and sink, next to the sitting room heated by local peat. Our hut was the other side of the toilet, with two iron bunk beds. Two of the men had brought their pet dogs which slept loose and outside - a Labrador and a Doberman.

After a good feed of sausage and mash and telling tales, we went our way to bed in the dark. I slept immediately - full of the Bell's whisky, to be woken in the dark by someone licking my face. I was alarmed, thinking that Gwyn Lloyd had changed his habits or his sex, only to find that he had gone out to urinate on the moors and had let the Labrador in. I was as relieved as he was! It was a lovely spot but on that occasion the brown trout fishing was poor. The experience was as exciting, but less civilised, than a week that Bob Owen and I had as guests of Dick Duncalf of Colwyn Bay. He spends six months of the year in a cottage on the side of a lake in County Mayo. He spoilt us, fed us and drove us in his fishing-dedicated van to his rowing boat. He would ghillie for us all day. We did well for the fish and marvelled at his generosity. I blotted my copybook twice as I splashed water over the bath through the sitting room ceiling and sat heavily at the kitchen table smashing a chair.

It was on a trip to Ireland a few years earlier that we went shark fishing from Kinsale, over the site where the Mauritania had been sunk by the Germans. Mari caught a 68lb shark from the fighting seat at the bow of the boat.

On one occasion she and I were fishing a river in Ireland near a mink farm when I caught my expensive minnow on a branch at the other side. It was too deep to cross in my waders; so I stripped completely and waded across, to be alarmed in the middle to see an escaped large mink swimming towards me. I kept my head and both my minnows!

Because of the difficulties in getting to patients, and to my home, I really hate the snow. Nevertheless when my daughter Elin wanted to go to Austria to ski with a girlfriend - now her sister-in-law Clare - Mari and I decided to go with them. One day, while they were on the slopes, we crossed the icy road in the mountainside village. I started to slide, then run down the icy road - only to crash into a shop step and down I went. I had already fractured the middle of my left upper arm in snow on our drive a couple of years before, when setting off to an injured neighbour, George Brookes. Now I knew immediately that the bone had gone again. I was taken to the local chromium-plated surgery with two good-looking nurses. The doctor x-rayed the shoulder - fractured. He sent for an ambulance to take me the 50 miles to the hospital, accompanied by Mari. I was not given anything for the pain. In the Casualty Department the furnishings looked crude. The anaesthetist was a nun, dressed in her nun's habit. She tried to find a vein to push in the general anaesthetic. She failed, so I pushed the needle in, then she pushed me to sleep. I woke later, my arm and chest in plaster of paris. Having got home at the end of the holiday I did not lose any days' work. I even did cervical smears while so handicapped! I had it x-rayed later and found the top of that bone to be in five pieces, so took myself to see my old friend Bob Owen, now the Professor of Orthopaedics in Liverpool. While looking at the films, a Mr Beddow, a world-expert on this joint, walked past and Bob asked his opinion. He asked me what I could not do. I told him that now I found it difficult to open my mack as I walk along the promenade in Rhyl on Saturday nights. He remained poker-faced. I hadn't realised he was a lay-preacher!

Drug firms, apart from taking us out locally to eat and advertise their wares, would take us abroad for weekends. One was to Jersey and we slept in the room in the Normandy Hotel, which Hitler had used. Another occasion was to the Hague and Amsterdam, where a few of the men went to experience a strip club.Bread and butter stuff to us!. Drug firms were responsible for breaking the barriers between practices in the town by their social activities. We are grateful to them.

Visits to London became almost commonplace when I was Chairman of the Royal College of GPs in Wales. On one occasion the President of the College, Dr Alistair Donald of Edinburgh, introduced me to Prince Charles, the patron, after the Prince had given a talk on the Health Service. I told the Prince that I had done a morning surgery in North Wales before coming up to London and told him that I was surprised that he knew so much about the Health Service. He voluntered that had had lots of staff to help him! I enquired of his fractured elbow. He replied that it ached in wet weather. I told him I was surprised, because even he, like everyone else, was 90 per cent water and what a little outside dampness could do puzzled me. He has a metal plate in the elbow. I warned him of lightning! As he laughed, his bodyguard led him to the next person and he said to remember him to my patients!

I was pleasantly surprised in 1989 to be invited through Bob Owen to be a General Practitioner to about 100 Surgeons and Anaesthetists from the Royal College of Surgeons of England, during their trip to Thailand and Malaya. It was a fantastic 2 weeks - banquets once or twice a day, meeting the King and Prime Minister of both countries, trips to the jungles, innumerable dancing girls, a beach and the famous railway over the River Kwai, where so many Allied soldiers were made to work and die in horrible conditions. I had only two patients; the wife of a surgeon had fits and I the squits. We stayed at the best hotels, fortunately with air conditioning, as well as did the coaches. I returned with hand-made, made-to-measure silk shirts at £10 each, and the name and address of the tailor in Bankok! Mari and I did not try the Tuck Tuck transport to the brothel area.

I was recently surprised when being introduced, as Chairman of the Gorsedd Committee, to the Duke of Edinburgh at a fund-raising dinner and ball for the Duke of Edinburgh Award Scheme in London, when he asked whether I was a Druid. I didn't think he would have known anything about the Eisteddfod. Two of our group of eight were farmers. He said that he was surprised that they could afford to travel there in these tough times. He didn't know that we had been flown there in a privately owned plane of a friend of ours!

I had been made a Druid - that is a white-robed member of the Gorsedd - for services to medical education in Wales, during the Eisteddfod in Machynlleth in 1982, with my family present. You don't have to be a poet! Mr Dafydd Wigley, MP (the recently retired President of Plaid Cymru) and I went to the Logan Stone together. It was quite a thrill and of course an honour. I try to attend all the Gorsedds in North Wales. Dressing with famous Welshmen and women is exciting - for example the late George Thomas, MP. Sir Geraint Evans took 15 minutes to arrange his head gear.

Although not a poet I enjoyed Dylan Thomas and sent a contribution to a memorial at Westminster Abbey. I was very surprised to receive an invitation for two to go to the dedication of the plaque, at the Abbey. Mari and our daughter Elin went up and sat behind Mr Harold Wilson, a former Prime Minister, and opposite one of the Churchills in the nave.

Elin came with Mari and myself to a Buckingham Palace garden party on one occasion. I had hired a suit. To my horror I found the thin trousers slipping down off the clips of the braces, as I stood chewing my cucumber sandwiches. Quickly, I put one hand in the trouser pocket to pull them up again and replace the clips at the back. We all enjoyed the experience of hob nobbing with royalty.

Although I was the Medical Students' representative, for the six years I was at the Medical School, I have not organised or wanted a reunion, for some reason. However, I have enjoyed the two reunions we have had of Denbigh County School pupils during the war years. Lord Emlyn Hooson was the ex-pupil guest on the second occasion and I was asked to thank him, publicly, for his speech. I said that I had always admired him since standing next to him in the boys' toilet! I then explained, when the mirth had settled, that it was because he was in his Naval uniform and come to see the Headmaster.

I was delighted to accept an invitation to be Father Christmas at Llanrhaeadr School, on one occasion in the last decade. I sat in the corner of the hall, with all the children seated around me. I had a sack with presents, prepared by the parents, by my side. The first I picked was for a little girl. As she walked towards me, I suddenly had a feeling of terror: "Am I going to kiss her (as I would have done previously) - or just shake her hand?" There had been so much about child abuse at the time. I settled for shaking her little hand when the boys shouted out, "Sws, sws!" (the Welsh for 'kiss, kiss') so I was happy to oblige - but had to kiss the teachers, cooks and cleaners as well!

By virtue of the large collection, perhaps 130, of old medical instruments I mentioned I have collected from my Grandfather, Father and others, I have appeared on four television programmes, two in Welsh and two in English. The more famous English one was with Trevor Fishlock as he toured the area. His wife phoned me yesterday enquiring how to spell my Christian name for a book he is writing. The more famous Welsh programme was Cefn Gwlad, with Dei Jones interviewing me. It took four days to prepare the programme, which lasted half-an-hour, on various aspects of my work and family. The team would arrive at 9 a.m. when we'd have coffee, talks and jokes around the kitchen table before the work. We visited a family 15 miles away on the Moors where it had taken me 8 hours to get a 4 week old child out in an incubator through thick snow on the ground, increasing with a further snow storm. Then we visited the Surgery, the Infirmary, Owen at work, and Elin in the Nursing Home. The programme put me in contact with very old Welsh friends.

Dei Jones and Trevor Fishlock are included in the list of the famous who have visited us - the President of the Royal College of General Practitioners from Edinburgh, with his wife, slept here. The most distinguished staying here must be Sir James Black, who recently was given the Order of Merit by the Queen, and a Nobel Prize, for his excellence in finding important, universally used drugs. He and his distinguished wife, a Professor of Dermatology, were attending a party locally in Dr Jane Wood's home. She, like Mr David Thomas the Gynaecologist before her, is Chairman of the Welsh Medical Committee but she is also Vice-Chairman of the General Medical Council UK Health Committee and a local Geriatrician. Another must be Graham Rees OBE, an old school friend, a nuclear physicist who helped develop the trigger of the hydrogen bomb, world famous in his sphere. His brother Colin came too.

I have been blessed with a wonderful, tolerant, clever wife and three fantastic children and, before two of them left home to be further educated in Cardiff just as Mari and I had been, we had happy holidays - for ten years in Abersoch, holding a string attached to an inflatable raft - doing what I always swore I never could do - copying my brother, who did it for a few years before - then we had 15 years in Newport, Pembrokeshire.

I learned more in a week in Israel than from going to Sunday School for ten years! We were walking in line, myself in front, through a narrow bazaar in Jerusalem when I spotted a local man looking admiringly at Elin. I turned around and warned them in Welsh to watch him. As Elin passed he pinched her bottom. I landed a heavy punch in his chest for his audacity!

Portugal, Greece, the Canary Islands and North Africa were our holiday destinations in a succession of years but the most interesting was when we hired a car at Kennedy Airport, New York, and drove through New York with enormous lorries passing each side of us and so South to Florida, calling at the Space Centre and the swamps. We met an old friend, a solicitor, Gwyn Williams and Norma, his wife. He took Mari and the children in his helicopter and we sat in the twin engine jet he shared with a colleague. As we sat one night at his poolside, with a whisky in our hands, he admitted that he would prefer to be in the Vale of Clwyd. He did return there for a year or so, before settling in South East England.

Mari and I went to India for about ten days - we never like going for longer anywhere. Like other visitors, we were nauseated by the degree of poverty there and compared it to the heavenly beauty of the Taj Mahal, then, a few years later, to the beauty and cleanliness of Iceland, amongst the icebergs. The whale watching was great. Another time, fishing the world-famous Campbell River, off the west coast of Canada, was a treat. We caught 24 Sock-eye salmon in the sea off the river, in one day. We were only allowed to keep 12, so the bald-headed eagles dived and collected the spare.

Recently, we both went to Pamplona in Northern Spain. I had seen the bulls loose in the street as a student, with my brother, and wanted to re-live it. I was on my knees with a camera at a barrier (between some lady's legs) trying to see the bulls galloping through behind the local, fearless lads. Mari had a better view. She refused to join me at the bullfight.

Soon after the threat of the Gulf War, we joined about 40 people from Cardiff, including our ex-Minister, Rev Cynwil Williams, for a tour of the Nile. I had a stock of anti-diarrhoea tablets with me, fortunately, and held a surgery on board the boat daily! Mari had to miss a whole day in the Valley of the Kings. I had taken a prophylactic tablet beforehand and was the only person in our group not to suffer.

At six o'clock one morning one of our group, a nurse, had been called to an English male tourist by his wife. He had been ill before starting from Yorkshire with some tummy trouble. The nurse called me and I found the man was dead. His wife had been given some injections to give him, by the local doctor in Aswan. He was taken off the boat in Cairo pretty roughly. The family wrote to me later.

In the last couple of years, I have shown interest in the Institute for Welsh Affairs and am now on the North Wales Executive. As far as I can see, one of the most important functions of the body is to ensure that South Wales does not monopolise everything and the evolution of a faster road or railway link from North to South Wales. Recently, I suggested that we dichotomise ourselves by using the words North and South, and that Northern and Southern would be less provocative and parochial.

I suppose that since I now play only a small part in medical politics, I get absorbed in local and national politics, though have never made a public speech on national politics. I enjoy gardening, especially the vegetables. Having 3 acres to care for takes more time, with the help of Teddy Thomas for the last 30 years. When I retired after 38 years I was happy to leave the Practice in the very capable and happy hands of the six doctors and Carys with the other staff.. I have enjoyed being President of the local Flower Show Committee for about 30 years. A lot of time is now taken up as Chairman of the Gorsedd Committee for the 2001 National Eisteddfod in Denbigh, and as Chairman of the North Wales Hospital Action Group, who are trying to save the derelict site for a park and nature trail for the town and Chairman of the Plas Madoc Fishing Syndicate on the Conway.

For the last few years I have been appointed a Spotter for my district for the Council for the Preservation of Rural Wales.

I never fail to say thank goodness that I was born to live here in Denbigh, with most of my family about me, and the beautiful Vale of Clwyd to enjoy.